Paul the Letter-Writer

His World, His Options, His Skills

Jerome Murphy-O'Connor, O.P.

A Michael Glazier Book

THE LITURGICAL PRESS
Collegeville, Minnesota

GOOD NEWS STUDIES

Volume 41

A Michael Glazier Book published by The Liturgical Press

Cover design by David Manahan, O.S.B.
St. Paul, mosaic fragment from old St. Peter's basilica; Vatican Grottoes.

1	2	3	4	5	6	7	8	9

Library of Congress Cataloging-in-Publication Data

Murphy-O'Connor, J. (Jerome), 1935–
    Paul the letter-writer : his world, his options, his skills / Jerome Murphy-O'Connor.
       p.   cm. — (Good news studies ; v. 41)
    "A Michael Glazier book."
    Includes bibliographical references and indexes.
    ISBN 0-8146-5845-8
    1. Bible. N.T. Epistles of Paul—Criticism, interpretation, etc.
2. Rhetoric in the Bible. I. Title. II. Series.
BS2650.2.M87   1995
227′.066—dc20   94-11566
                                   CIP

Contents

Introduction

The purpose of this book is to do for the Pauline letters what my *St. Paul's Corinth* did for the the great city, which had been the Apostle's missionary base for eighteen months and whose Church gave him more trouble than any other. There I compiled the classical references which restored Corinth's specific identity by revealing how it worked and how visitors perceived it. Here I want to concretize the letters by setting them in their first-century context and by highlighting their individuality.

In the first chapter I deal with the writing of a first-century letter, in terms both of the raw materials (pen, ink, and paper) and of the actual composition and presentation. This involves a discussion of Paul's use of secretaries and coauthors. Throughout I quote as much as possible of the contemporary data.

The second chapter focuses on the formal features of all the letters, with the exception of Hebrews. The emphasis is not on their content, but on the way the material is organized. A synoptic survey of the beginnings and ends of the letters brings out the extent to which Paul adapted current epistolary conventions, while at the same time drawing attention to his mood while writing and to his relations with the recipients. The body of the letter is dealt with from the perspectives of both rhetorical and epistolary criticism. In both cases I explain these modern approaches to the letters and evaluate their advantages and disadvantages.

The last chapter is concerned with the formation of the Pauline canon and attempts to answer the question: How were the letters, which the Apostle wrote to widely scattered Churches, brought together to create a single collection?

Even though some of the discussions may be a little involved, this is a book for beginners. To confront Paul's thought is a daunting task at which many take fright. If, through an investigation of apparently banal extrinsic details, the letters are seen as intensely human documents, readers are less likely to be put off by the the complexity of Paul's theology.

I dedicate this book to my colleagues and students at the École Biblique, where I have now taught for twenty-five years. Their generous cooperation in the partnership of the quest for truth has been a source of stimulation and support for which I can never adequately express my gratitude. My particular thanks are due to Anthony Ward, S.M., and Paolo Garuti, O.P., who read the manuscript and made many helpful suggestions. Any faults that remain are my responsibility.

Jerome Murphy-O'Connor, O.P.
École Biblique de Jérusalem

1

Putting Pen to Paper

This chapter is concerned with the mechanics of writing and sending a letter in the Greco-Roman world in which Paul lived and worked. After dealing with the most basic requirements of paper, pen, and ink, we shall look at the qualifications and use of secretaries. The speed and efficiency of a secretary obviously had an influence on a writer's style and method of work—less so, however, than the interventions of coauthors who had more control over the subject matter. At each stage, after explaining and illustrating the point at issue, its relevance for understanding the Pauline letters will be examined.

THE TOOLS OF A WRITER'S TRADE

In reponse to a letter from his brother, Quintus, Cicero wrote in July 54 B.C.:

> For this letter I shall use a good pen, well-mixed ink, and ivory-polished paper too. For you write that you could hardly read my last letter, but for that there were none of those reasons which you suspect my dear brother. I was not busy, nor upset, nor angry with someone, but it is always my practice to use whatever pen I find in my hand as if it were a good one (*QFr* 2:15b.1; Williams).

Pen, ink, and paper were the essential prerequisites for any written document. Without one of the three nothing could be done. Thus, gifts were sent both to shame tardy correspondents and to facilitate their response, as Terentianus did to his sister Tasoucharion: "I sent papyrus to you in order that you would be able to write to me about your health" (*PMich* VIII, 481; White 1986, 177).

The rather primitive nature of the components, however, meant that writers of antiquity needed more equipment than their modern counterparts. Two poems list what the competent scribe required.

> Callimenes, resting from its long labour his sluggish hand
>   that trembles with age, dedicates to Hermes,
> his disc of lead that running correctly close
>   to the straight ruler can deftly mark its track,
> the hard steel that eats the pens,
> the ruler itself, guide of the undeviating line,
> the rough stone on which the double-tooth of the pen
>   is sharpened when blunted by long use,
> the sponge, wandering Triton's couch in the deep,
>   healer of the pen's errors,
> and the ink-box with many cavities that holds in one
>   all the implements of calligraphy.
>   (*Greek Anthology* 6:65; Paton 1939)

> A lead disc composed of black stuff for marking,
> A ruler, the officer who keeps the lines straight,
> The holder of the stream of black writing ink,
> His well-cut pens split at the top,
> An abrasive stone which regulates the worn-down pens,
> To give definition to the characters when they are rough,
> His penknife, a broad pointed metal spear—
> These things, the tools of his trade, dedicates
> Menedemus, on his retirement, his old eyes growing dim,
> To Hermes. Take care of your craftsman.
>   (*Greek Anthology* 6:63; Jay 1981)

As these poems show, the reed pen (*calamus*) remained standard throughout antiquity. The earliest existing metal pens are dated to the third or fourth centuries A.D.,[1] and the first reference to a pen made from a bird's feather (*penna*) appears in the seventh century A.D.[2] Martial thought that the best reeds for pens came from Egypt.

> Bundles of Pens
> The land of Memphis supplies reeds handy for writing;
> Let your roof be thatched with the reeds of other marshes.
>
> (*Epigrams* 14:38; Ker)

Pliny the Elder was not entirely convinced:

> Reeds serve as pens for writing on paper, and especially the Egyptian reeds owing to their kinship, as it were, with papyrus; although the reeds of Cnidus and those that grow around the Anaetic lake in Asia are more esteemed (*Natural History* 16:157; Rackham).[3]

A sharp knife was used to shape one end of a section of the reed to a point which it then split. When the nib began to fray, the superfluous fibers were rubbed off on a stone. In time complete deterioration was inevitable, but then the old nib was simply chopped off and a new one shaped. Carving a new nib economically and quickly was not a skill that all possessed.

Red ink was used for decorating initials or titles, as in a copy of Numbers among the Dead Sea Scrolls (4QNum b), but the standard ink was jet black. The essential ingredient for this was soot, the carbon deposit scraped from the inside of a chimney. It was suspended in a solution of gum water in a metal or ceramic holder (Forbes 1955, 228). Bronze and earthenware inkwells were

---

[1]Crinagoras (70 B.C.–?A.D. 20) wrote a poem to accompany a birthday present: "This silver pen-nib with its newly polished holder, nicely mounted with two easily dividing tips, running glib with even flow over the rapidly written page . . ." (*Greek Anthology* 6:227). The extravagance of the gesture does not guarantee that the pen was ever used.

[2]"Feder," PW 6:2099–100.

[3]Cnidus is a peninsula projecting from the southwest corner of modern Turkey opposite the island of Rhodes. The Anaetic lake is in Armenia near the Euphrates.

found in the settlement at Qumran which produced the Dead Sea
Scrolls (de Vaux 1973, 29–30). If the writer made a mistake it could
be erased by a damp sponge before the ink dried. The sponge also
served to clean the pen after work; "the sponge he used to wipe
his Cnidian pens" (*Greek Anthology* 6:295).

The English word *paper* is derived via Old French from the
Latin *papyrus,* itself simply the transcription of the Greek
papyros, which was the name of a plant (*Cyperus papyrus*) that
grew in the swamps of Egypt or in shallow stagnant pools left
by the fall of the Nile after the flood season. The plant has a root
as thick as a person's arm and tapers gracefully up with triangu-
lar sides to a height of some ten feet. The most detailed ancient
history of the use of such papyrus stalks in the manufacture of
paper is given by Pliny the Elder in his *Natural History* 13:68–83,
from which the following quotations are taken.[4]

> The process of making paper from papyrus is to split it with
> a needle into very thin strips as wide as possible. The best qual-
> ity is in the centre of the plant, and so on in order of its split-
> ting up. . . . (§74)
>
> Paper of all kinds is "woven" on a board moistened with
> water from the Nile mixed with glue. First an upright layer is
> smeared on to the table, using the full length of papyrus avail-
> able after the trimmings have been cut off at both ends, and
> afterwards cross strips complete the lattice work. The next step
> is to press it in presses, and the sheets are dried in the sun and
> then joined together. . . . There are never more than 20 sheets
> in a roll. . . . (§77)
>
> The common kind of paste for paper is made of fine flour
> of the best quality mixed with boiling water, because carpenter's
> paste and gum make too brittle a compound. A more careful
> process is to strain the crumbs of unleavened bread in boiling
> water. This method requires the smallest amount of paste at
> the seams, and produces a paper softer even than linen. But
> all the paste used ought to be exactly a day old—no more, no
> less. Afterward the paper is beaten thin with a mallet and run

[4]The translation is essentially that of H. Rackham in the Loeb Classical
Library. The full text is also given in Barrett (1987, 24–28).

over with a layer of paste, and then again has its creases removed by pressure and is flattened out with the mallet (§82).

The basic characteristics sought in paper were, according to Pliny, "fineness, stoutness, whiteness and smoothness" (§78). Their variation gave rise to different qualities of paper, each, he tells us, associated with a different width. The best paper was 13 Roman inches wide (= 9.75 modern inches or 24.7 cm)—standardized by the emperor Claudius to 12 Roman inches (= 9 modern inches or 22.86 cm)—whereas poor paper measured 9 Roman inches (= 6.75 modern inches or 17 cm) (§78). For the sake of comparison, standard American paper is 8.5 inches wide (= 21.5 cm) and European A4 paper slightly less (8.25 inches wide or 21 cm).

The sheet of paper was prepared for writing by smoothing it with a piece of ivory or a shell. Pliny notes that this had to be done with great care because if the paper was given too high a shine it did not take the ink well (§81). Hence some preferred to use pumice stone; "his pumice for smoothing" (*Greek Anthology* 6:295; cf. 6:62). The next step was to mark the margins with a circular lead which left a faint but unambiguous trace. It also served to rule the lines on which the letters stood.[5]

In the text from Pliny cited above mention is made of joining sheets of papyrus to create a roll. Fifty sheets or so could also be stacked, folded across the center, and fastened along that line to create a gathering or quire. This was a much cheaper version of the parchment codex made of "many-folded skins" (Martial 14:184; cf. 14:185-192). An effort was made to have facing pages exhibit the same side of the papyrus. Vertical strips on the left page were matched by vertical strips on the right page; the following pages necessarily had horizontal strips.

The earliest surviving collection of Paul's letters is the Chester Beatty Papyrus (P46). Written about A.D. 200, this is a codex of 52 papyrus sheets folded once to create 104 pages, each with 24 lines. Unfortunately not all have survived. The fact that the pages

[5]The opposite is true of Hebrew manuscrips where the letters hang from the ruled line. In consequence, photographs of such manuscripts are sometimes printed upside down.

are numbered on the top shows that seven pages are missing at the beginning; a similar number must be missing at the end. This codex contained all the letters with the exception of 1 and 2 Timothy and Titus (Finegan 1956, 92–93).

Paul Used a Secretary

Although Paul composed his letters, both independently and with others, he did not personally commit them to paper. Most letter writers in antiquity used a professional secretary and the Apostle was no exception (Eschlimann 1946, Bahr 1966, Richards 1991). Cicero sometimes explicitly mentions at the beginning of a letter that he is dictating:

> I don't think you ever before read a letter of mine which I had not written myself (*Att* 2:23.1; Winstedt).
> The bare fact that my letter is by the hand of a secretary will show you how busy I am (*Att* 4:16.1; Winstedt).
> This letter is dictated as I sit in my carriage on my road to the camp (*Att* 5:17.1; Winstedt).

Paul never makes such explicit statements. Nonetheless the fact is beyond question.

The secretary to whom Paul dictated Romans makes his presence obvious in the note, "I, Tertius, the writer of this letter, greet you in the Lord" (Rom 16:23). This is the only case in which one of the apostle's secretaries intervenes personally and identifies himself. That he felt free to do so says much for his relationship to Paul; no professional hired for the occasion would have taken the liberty. Tertius was more a friend and collaborator than an employee. In this regard Richards (1991, 170) very appositely evokes Cicero's allusion to the secretary of his friend Atticus:

> I am pleased that Alexis so often sends greetings to me; but why cannot he put them in a letter of his own, as Tiro, who is my Alexis, does for you (*Att* 5:20.9; Winstedt).

A confidential secretary is almost an extension of his master's personality.

In other letters Paul betrays the presence of a secretary by drawing attention to a change in handwriting: "I, Paul, write this greeting with my own hand (*tē emē cheiri*). This is the mark in every letter of mine" (2 Thess 3:17); "See with what large letters I have written to you with my own hand" (Gal 6:11); "The greeting [is] in my own hand, [the hand] of Paul" (1 Cor 16:21); "I, Paul, have written this with my own hand" (Phlm 19); "The greeting [is] in my own hand, [the hand] of Paul" (Col 4:18). Richards (1991, 173 and 176–77, against Bahr, 1968) notes that in antiquity such references occur at the beginning of the autograph section, and thus denies that the aorist *egrapsa*, "I have written," in Galatians and Philemon refers to the entire letters, as some have argued. A concluding paragraph, normally brief, in the author's handwriting showed that he had checked the final draft and assumed responsibility.

What about the other letters? Was a secretary used in 2 Corinthians, Philippians, and 1 Thessalonians? A favorable presumption is generated by Paul's practice as evidenced by the six letters mentioned above. And a strong argument can be made for 1 Thessalonians and 2 Corinthians.

Richards draws attention to the facts (1) that the content of 1 Thessalonians 5:27-28 parallels that of the authenticating postscript in 2 Thessalonians 3:17-18, and (2) that the formulation ("this is the mark in every letter I write") implies that Paul had done something similar previously. Moreover, while 1 Thessalonians is written in the first person plural, the first person singular appears at the very end of the letter (1 Thess 5:27). Richards (1991, 189 n. 281), therefore, rightly considers secretarial help probable for 1 Thessalonians.

Richards assigns the same qualification to 2 Corinthians, but his arguments here are not convincing. He treats 2 Corinthians 10–13 as a postscript, but manifestly these chapters cannot be considered a postscript in the same sense as those in 1 and 2 Thessalonians; they are in fact an independent letter which was subsequently tacked on to another letter, namely 2 Corinthians 1–9 (Murphy-O'Connor 1990, 50:2-3). Moreover, Richards fails to note the shift from the first person plural to the first person singular in 2 Corinthians 9:1 (see below, p. 28), and the parallel between this chapter and Galatians 6:11-18. In my view this suggests that 2 Corinthians 9 should be considered a personal post-script authenticating 2 Corinthians 1–8. If this is correct, 2 Corinthians 1–8 was also written by a secretary.

Nothing, in Richards' view, can be ascertained concerning Philippians. The reason is probably related to its character as a collection of three originally independent letters. In my opinion (1966) it is a combination of three epistles (*Letter A*: 1:3–3:1 and 4:2-9; *Letter B:* 3:2–4:1; *Letter C:* 4:10-20). In being assembled they may have undergone an editorial process in which the autograph sections were omitted because authenticity was not a problem and/or the content of these sections was deemed insignificant.

In order to answer the question of how Paul employed his secretary, we have to look first at the various possibilities. How were secretaries used in the first century? The response, of course, depends on how skilled they were.

FIRST-CENTURY SECRETARIES AND THEIR SKILLS

The evidence accumulated by Richards shows that in the first century secretaries functioned as recorders, as editors, and as substitute authors.

Recorder

In the Greco-Roman world all who went to school learned to write, and were trained by being obliged to take down dictation, a tradition that remained part of many Western educational systems until the mid-twentieth century. Thus any educated person could become the recorder of the words of another provided that they were spoken slowly. Cicero said on one occasion, "I dictated it to Spintharus syllable by syllable" (*Att* 13:25.3). For those without the imagination to perceive how slow and laborious this was, the inconvenience is well brought out by Quintilian (ca. A.D. 35–ca. 95).

> If the secretary is a slow writer, or lacking in intelligence, he becomes a stumbling-block, our speed is checked, and the thread of our ideas is interrupted by the delay or even perhaps by the

loss of temper to which it gives rise (*Institutio Oratoria* 10:3.20; Butler).

For busy people the method became effective only when the gaps created by the secretary having to spell out the words could be filled. One option is illustrated by the practice of Julius Caesar. According to Pliny,

> He used to write or read and dictate or listen simultaneously, and to dictate to his secretaries four letters at once on his important affairs or, if otherwise unoccupied, seven letters at once (*Natural History* 7:91; Rackham).

Obviously, only an excellent memory and total concentration could permit Caesar to function like this. Most were not so fortunate.

Inevitably there was pressure for the development of a system of shorthand capable of attaining the speed of normal speech. The pedantic term is *tachygraphy* (from *tacheia,* "fast" and *graphē,* "writing") but the earliest attestation of *tachygraphos,* "shorthand writer," appears in the sixth century A.D. (LSJ 1966, 1762a). Plutarch (ca. A.D. 46–ca. 120) uses the synonym *sēmiographos,* "sign writer" (*Cato Minor* 23:5).

Latin shorthand was certainly in use in the middle of the first century A.D. In a letter written in A.D. 63–64 Seneca, listing the inventions of slaves, says,

> What about signs for whole words, which enable us to take down a speech, however rapidly uttered, matching speed of tongue by speed of hand (*celeritatem linguae manus sequitur*)? (*Ep* 90:25; Gummere).[6]

Some time in the last third of the first century A.D. Martial wrote,

> Quick as speech is, the hand is quicker;/Before the tongue stops, the hand has finished (*Epigrams* 14:208).

[6]According to Eusebius (*Chronica* 156) and Isidor (*Etmologiae* 1:22.1.) the slave in question was Marcus Tullius Tiro, the freedman, secretary and friend of Cicero; for further details, see Richards (31 n. 77).

Quintilian confirms the widespread use of speed dictation by emphasizing its dangers.

> The condemnation which I have passed on such carelessness in writing will make it pretty clear what my views are on the luxury of dictation, which is now so fashionable. For, when we write, however great our speed, the fact that the hand cannot follow the rapidity of our thoughts gives us time to think, whereas the presence of our amanuensis hurries us on, and at times we feel ashamed to hesitate or pause, or make some alteration, as though we were afraid to display such weakness before a witness. As a result, our language tends not merely to be haphazard and formless, but in our desire to produce a continuous flow, we let slip positive improprieties of diction, which show neither the precision of the writer nor the impetuosity of the speaker (*Institutio Oratoria* 10:3.19-20; Butler).

Here it is certainly question of secretaries who can keep up with the pace of normal speech. Are some of the faults in Paul's letters to be attributed to intimidation by a skilled, professional secretary?

A strong-minded author, however, had little difficulty dealing with the problem. Pliny the Younger describes his technique:

> If I have anything on hand I work it out in my head, choosing and correcting the wording, and the amount I achieve depends on the ease or difficulty with which my thoughts can be marshalled and kept in my head. Then I call my secretary, the shutters are opened, and, I dictate to him what I have put into shape; he goes out, is recalled, and again dismissed (*Letters* 9:36.2; Radice).

The relevance of these references to Latin shorthand for the case of Paul, who wrote in Greek, is that the well-established Roman practice of his day was borrowed. Plutarch gives the credit to Cicero (106–43 B.C.) for introducing shorthand to Rome.

> This is the only speech of Cato which has been preserved, we are told, and its preservation was due to Cicero the consul, who had previously given to those clerks who excelled in rapid writ-

ing instruction in the use of signs, which, in small and short figures, comprised the force of many letters; these clerks he had then distributed in various parts of the senate-house. For up to that time the Romans did not employ or even possess what are called shorthand writers, but then for the first time, we are told, the first steps towards the practice were taken (*Cat Min* 23:3-5; Perrin).

Where did Cicero learn the technique? The only possible answer is in Greece. He had lived there and in Greek-speaking Asia for three years (79–76 B.C.) and he both spoke and wrote Greek, as did his secretary, Tiro (Bailey 1971; Rawson 1975). His letters contain a multitude of citations in Greek. Richards (1991, 36–37) most plausibly conjectures that Tiro did not create Latin shorthand from nothing, but, using his secretarial experience, he merely adapted the Greek system to Latin, and that Cicero then propagated it.

This line of argument suggests that there was already a developed Greek shorthand system in the first century B.C. The earliest surviving Greek stenographic report, however, dates from over a century later, namely, Arrian's (ca. A.D. 96–180) record of the classes of Epictetus (ca. A.D. 50–120). The evidence is indirect; the discourses, which of course have been transcribed, differ in language, style, spirit, and tempo from the works that Arrian composed in his own name (Richards 1991, 36–37). As far as we know at present, the oldest collection of a series of Greek stenographic symbols is to be found in an early second century A.D. rcuscd forty-line manuscript from the Wadi Murabba'at in Palestine (*PMur* 164; Benoit et al, 275–79); no one so far has worked out the precise meaning of the symbols.

The use of papyrus for taking down shorthand must have been exceptional, because it implied the use of a pen. The need to dip the pen in the inkwell and shake off surplus ink would have been an obstacle to speed. Were the speaker's pauses coordinated with the the number of words a pen could write with one dip of ink, the secretary could keep up. Such mutual understanding, however, could not be taken for granted. It must have been much more common for dictation to be taken down on wax-covered wooden tablets wired together; the pointed stylus could incise letters indefinitely at speed. At the secretary's leisure the shorthand symbols were later written out in normal letters on parchment or papyrus.

The spread of shorthand, which can hardly have appeared *de novo* in the early second century A.D., is confirmed by a document dated A.D. 155 from Egypt.

> Panechotes also called Panares, ex-cosmetes of Oxyrhynchus, through his friend Gemellus, to Apollonius, writer of shorthand [*sēmeiographos*] greeting.
>
> I have placed with you my slave Chaerammon to be taught the signs which your son Dionysius knows, for a period of two years dating from the present month Phamenoth of the 18th year of Antoninus Caesar the lord, at the salary agreed upon between us, 120 drachmae, not including feast days; of which sum you have received the first instalment amounting to 40 drachmae, and you will receive the second instalment consisting of 40 drachmae when the boy has learnt the whole system, and the third you will receive at the end of the period when the boy writes fluently in every respect and reads faultlessly, viz. the remaining 40 drachmae.
>
> If you make him perfect within the period, I will not wait for the aforesaid limit; but it is not lawful for me to take the boy away before the end of the period, and he shall remain with you after the expiration of it for as many days or months as he may have done no work.
>
> The 18th year of the Emperor Caesar Titus Aelius Hadrianus Antoninus Augustus Pius, Phamenoth 5 (*POxy* 724; Richards 1991, 38).

The implications of this contract are spelled out by Richards: "Although this text is from the mid-second century, a reasonable period of development that allows for proliferation to provincial Egypt and the establishment of an apprenticeship system requires a flourishing practice of Greek shorthand in the first century" (1991, 39).

It was normal practice for a copy of a letter to be retained by the sender. The author could make it himself (Cicero, *Fam* 9:26.1), but the copying was normally the work of the secretary; this is the implication of Cicero's criticism of a friend for personally making his own copies (*Fam* 7:18.2). Copies of all Cicero's correspondence were kept by Tiro, as we know from a letter to Atticus:

> You ask for my letter to Brutus. I have not a copy: but there is one in existence and Tiro says you ought to have it: and, so far as I recollect, I sent you my answer along with his letter of reproof (*Att* 13:6.3; Winstedt).

This passage indicates that a personal archive, both for control and perhaps future use,[7] was not the only reason why copies were made. Letters were shared with friends.

Thus far, the secretary has been discussed in terms of outgoing material, but he could also play a role in respect to incoming data. The secretary recorded material for the future use of the author. The younger Pliny mentions a habit of his uncle:

> In his journeys, as though released from all other cares, he gave every minute to study; he kept at his side a secretary with book and tablets [*notarius cum libro et pugillaribus*] (*Letters* 3:5.15; Radice).

The secretary read aloud to his master and, when requested, recorded excerpts. When Pliny the Elder died he bequeathed his nephew "160 notebooks of selected passages, written in a minute hand on both sides of the page, so that their number is really doubled" (*Letters* 3:5.17; Radice). Clearly here it is question of parchment codices, which at that time were in the process of replacing tablets. These were thin pieces of wood covered with wax and wired together in batches of two, three, five, or more (Richards 1991, 164).

Editor

The secretary sometimes served merely as a copyist. Yet he could be entrusted with a slightly greater degree of responsibility. The

---

[7]Richards (1991, 5) shows that Cicero was not above using the same good line in letters to different people; compare *Fam* 10:28.1 and *Fam* 12:4.1.

author could permit the secretary to make minor changes in the form or content of the letter when preparing the final text from the rough dictation copy or from a preliminary draft prepared by the author himself.

This sort of thing is perfectly illustrated by an exchange between Cicero and his secretary Tiro. The latter became ill when away from Cicero, who wrote to tell him to look after himself and not to return until he had recovered (*Fam* 16:22). In his reply Tiro must have given an assurance that he would "faithfully" care for his health, because Cicero picks him up for the incorrect use of the adverb.

> *Sed heus tu, qui* kanōn *esse meorum scriptorum soles, unde illud tam* akyron *"valetudini fideliter inserviendo"*? But look you here, sir, you who love to be the "rule" of my writings, where did you get such a solecism as "faithfully ministering to your health"? (*Fam* 16:17.1; Williams).[8]

Despite the good-humoured tone, Cicero is obviously delighted to have the opportunity of correcting his corrector. The implication is that it was part of Tiro's function to correct slips made by Cicero and to ensure the accuracy of the finished work. In a word, he acted as a modern copy editor, who points out errors and asks if a particular formulation really conveys precisely what the author wanted to say.

Substitute Author

The secretary's responsibilities could be even more extensive. He could be trusted not only to supervise the form of a letter but also to create its content. He could be ordered to compose a suitable letter and to send it in his employer's name.

Once again Cicero provides a case in point, although the recipient of his request in this instance is his closest friend Atticus, and not a mere secretary. Banished from Rome in 58 B.C. for

---

[8]Note the presence of two Greek words in the Latin text which underline the bilingualism of both Cicero and Tiro: *kanōn*, "rule, standard"; *akyros*, "improper, invalid."

refusing to bow to the Triumvirs, Cicero wrote from Thessalonica to ensure that he would not be forgotten at home, "If there is anyone to whom you think a letter ought to be sent in my name, please write one and see that it is sent" (*Att* 3:15.8; Winstedt).

It is not clear whether Cicero intended any deception in this case. He may have presumed that Atticus would indicate that he was writing by order of Cicero. The situation was very different some ten or twelve years later. He again wrote to Atticus:

> I am so fearfully upset both in mind and body that I have not been able to write many letters; I have answered only those who have written to me. I should like you to write in my name to Basilius and to anyone else you like, even to Servilius, and say whatever you think fit (*Att* 11:5; cf. 11:3; Winstedt).

Here there is a definite element of deception, although to a great extent it is excused by the author's bone-deep weariness with life. Richards (1991, 50, 108) correctly infers from the following instruction to Atticus that Cicero wanted to make it appear that the letters came from him personally. "If they look for my [missing] seal or handwriting, say that I have avoided them because of the guards" (*Att* 11:2.4; Winstedt).

Cicero apparently was perfectly capable of repaying the favor. The implications of a remark of his, "I read him your letter—no, the letter of your secretary" (*Att* 6:6.4), has given rise to some discussion. A plausible reconstruction of the circumstances postulates that Cicero dictated a letter addressed to himself using the secretary of Atticus. The letter contained words of praise for Caelius Caldus. Desiring to put Atticus in Caelius' good graces, Cicero then read the letter to Caelius, as if it had come from Atticus (Richards 1991, 110). The degree of deception here is much more serious. Even though the gesture was inspired by friendship, the letter had not been authorized by Atticus. That Cicero felt pangs of conscience may be deduced from the fact that he eventually told Atticus what he had done.

Only a close friend could have guessed what Cicero would want to say or would be likely to say to his acquaintances. Equally Cicero would have had to be very sure of the feelings of Atticus. In neither case was the matter such as could be left to a detached professional secretary. This fact, when coupled with the element of deception, makes the occasional practice of Cicero (from whom all the available evidence comes) unrepresentative of secretarial practice in the first century (Richards 1991, 111).

Many letters, however, were more impersonal. An employee could author letters which were no more than formal acknowledgements or submissions. The convention deceived no one. The commissioned collection of data also belongs to this category. M. Celius Rufus had promised to keep the exiled Cicero informed of all that was going on in Rome. Not having time to do it himself, he hired a secretary to compose a digest of official decrees, gossip, and rumors, which turned out to be so long that Rufus did not have time to look it over personally. The fact that he told Cicero exactly what he had done excludes any deception (in point of fact it is not known if it was sent in Rufus' own name) and implies acceptance of responsibility (*Fam* 8:1.1).

COLLABORATORS AS COAUTHORS

Paul mentions one or more associates in the address of a number of letters.

1 Thess	Silvanus and Timothy
2 Thess	Silvanus and Timothy
1 Cor	Sosthenes the brother
2 Cor	Timothy the brother
Phil	Timothy
Phlm	Timothy the brother
Gal	All the brethren with me
Col	Timothy the brother

In the remainder of the letters (namely, Rom, Eph, 1–2 Tim, and Titus), Paul appears alone.

It is customary to treat these two groups of letters as if there were no difference. The Fathers saw in the mention of others only evidence of Paul's courtesy and modesty. He mentioned those in his company as he began to write; a gracious but meaningless gesture. Modern commentators, on the contrary, have tended to discuss such associates in terms of their special relationship to the communities addressed. Silvanus and Timothy, we are reminded, had been part of the team which founded the church at Thessalonica. Sosthenes had once been a member of the Corinthian community. As Paul's closest collaborator, Timothy was well known and deeply appreciated in all the communities (so Harnack 1926, 12, to be followed by many).

There is some contemporary evidence for the inclusion in the address of individuals who have a special relationship to the recipient. Cicero includes his son Marcus in the address of letters to his wife and daughter (*Fam* 14:14, 18). But when he writes to his wife alone, greetings from Marcus are included and he is not named in the address (*Fam* 14:5, 7). A series of letters to Tiro, written between 2 November 50 B.C. and 12 January 49 B.C., come from Cicero and his son together with his brother Quintus and the latter's son (*Fam* 16:1, 3, 4, 5, 6); in one letter all these are joined by Cicero's wife and daughter: "Tullius and Cicero, Terentia, Tullia, Quintus and Quintus greet Tiro a hundred times" (*Fam* 16:11). It is noteworthy that in this series, when one or other are absent for even a day they are not included in the address. Thus *Fam* 16:2 is sent by Cicero alone, and *Fam* 16:7 and 9 by Cicero and Marcus, because Quintus and his son were elsewhere (cf. *Fam* 16:3, 7). Despite the occasional use of "we" in a number of these letters, the predominance of "I" makes it clear that Cicero alone is the author (Prior 1989, 178 n. 6).

The relevance of these parallels to Paul's epistles is severely diminished by the fact that both recipients are especially significant members of Cicero's household, his wife and closest associate. The Pauline letters are addressed to communities. They belong to a different category from Cicero's highly personal letters to Terentia and Tiro. What is important, however, is that Cicero mentions *all* those with him who have a relationship to the recipient, even when this makes for an extremely cumbersome address.

This is not the case with Paul. Prisca and Aquila were with the apostle when he wrote 1 Corinthians (16:19), as was Titus when he wrote 2 Corinthians 1–9 (8:6). The couple had a claim to be founders of the church of Corinth insofar as they were in Corinth prior to Paul and were not converted by him (Acts 18:2-3; Lampe 1992, 1:319). Titus had been instrumental in the resolution of a dangerous crisis in the relations of the Corinthian church with Paul (2 Cor 7:6-7). If companions such as these are passed over in silence, it means that a relationship to the community addressed was not Paul's criterion of selection for mention in the address.

Implicit in both the ancient and modern approaches to the question of multiple senders is the assumption that the inclusion of others in the address of letters in fact written by an individual was nothing exceptional in antiquity. Recent studies, however, do not bear this out. Pliny, Seneca, and Cicero, Richards (1991, 47 n. 138) asserts,[9] never name anyone else in the address, nor, it may be added, does Ignatius of Antioch. Cicero nonetheless was aware of the possibility of a cooperative letter, because he once wrote to Atticus, "For my part I perceived from your letters both those which you have written jointly with others [*quas communiter cum aliis*] and those in your own name [*quas tuo nomine*] what I had already guessed would be the case, that you are as it were unnerved by the unexpectedness of what has happened and are casting around for new ways of protecting me" (*Att* 11:5.1; Bailey, n. 76). The fact that he raised the point, however, hints that epistolary coauthorship was unusual.

This inference is confirmed by research into letters with multiple named senders. In order to maintain the parallel with the bulk of the Pauline letters, I exclude letters addressed by a group (e.g., *1 Clement,* "The church of God transiently sojourning in Rome"; cf. 1 Macc 14:20; 2 Macc 1:1, 10) or by a named figure and unnamed others (e.g., Polycarp, *Phil,* "Polycarp and the elders with him" [cf. 1 Macc 12:5 = Josephus, *AJ* 13:163], even though this latter is parallel to Gal.).

Prior (1989, 38) found only fifteen papyrus letters with multiple named senders, whereas Richards (1991, 47 n. 138) discovered that only six out of 645 papyrus letters from Oxyrhynchus, Tebtunis, and Zenon had a plurality of senders. Such a tiny proportion indicates that the naming of another person in the address was anything but a meaningless convention (Roller 1933, 153). In fact to name others was especially significant, and, as one might have expected, multiple sender letters are formulated

[9]This needs to be corrected in the light of what has been said above regarding Cicero's letters to his wife and to Tiro.

exclusively in the first person plural (e.g., the letter of the three Roman officials [2 Macc 11:34-38] and the petition of the twins Thaues and Taous [White 1986, 68–70]).[10]

Such contemporary data suggests that the mention of those associated with Paul in the address should be explained in terms of the letter; that is, he selected them to play a role in the creation of the epistle as coauthors. It seems obvious that the recipients of such letters would have taken the "we" at face value as referring to the senders (Roller 1933, 170).

1 and 2 Thessalonians

A number of commentators have had no difficulty in granting Silvanus and Timothy a substantive role in the composition of 1 and 2 Thessalonians (J. Weiss 1910, 2; Frame 1912, 68; Bruce 1982, xi, 6; Fee 1987, 30; Prior 1989, 40). Their justification is the consistent use of "we" in both letters. Even though the first person singular intrudes on a number of occasions—three times in 1 Thessalonians (2:18; 3:5; 5:27) and twice in 2 Thessalonians (2:5; 3:17)—each case is adequately explained as a necessarily personal interjection into a joint letter on the part of Paul, exercising his prerogative as leader (so rightly Askwith 1911; Prior 1989, 40). Paul emphasizes his affection for the Thessalonians (1 Thess 2:18; 3:5), reminds them of what he had told them on a crucial point (2 Thess 2:5), and finally authenticates the letters written by a secretary (1 Thess 5:27; 2 Thess 3:17; Richards 1991, 189 n. 281).

The highly personal character of the "I" passages in fact strengthens the communal character of the letter as a whole. Failure to note this point explains C.E.B. Canfield's view that in the Thessalonian correspondence the first person plural should be interpreted in the light of the first person singular. He also draws

[10]The shift in the Pauline letters from first person singular to first person plural and vice versa has been the object of a number of studies, notably Dobschütz and Lofthouse. Prior's (1989, 44 n. 22) trenchant criticism of Lofthouse is very much to the point. Detailed statistics on the use of "I" and "we" are provided by Roller (1933, 168–87) but his discussion of coauthorship remains on the level of the letters as complete entities.

attention to 1 Thessalonians 3:2, which Harnack (1926, 12) considered the decisive refutation of joint authorship, because according to this hypothesis Timothy would send himself (so recently Furnish 1984, 103). Common sense disposes of this forced objection; it is perfectly feasible for a group to dispatch one of its members on a mission, as university faculties and parliaments demonstrate with great regularity. No doubt in practice the initiative came from Paul (1 Thess 3:5) and Silvanus and Timothy concurred (Frame 1912, 121; Bruce 1982, 61).

First Corinthians

Our conclusion regarding the joint authorship of 1 and 2 Thessalonians in turn creates a prima facie case that 1 Corinthians was also coauthored, since Paul there names Sosthenes in the address (1:1). This assumption, however, is immediately contradicted by the use of "I" in the thanksgiving (1:4) which signals the predominance of the first person singular in the rest of the letter. Commentators vary widely in their treatment of this problem. Conzelmann (1975, 20 n. 12) insists that "the fellow-writer is not a fellow-author," whereas Merklein (1992, 68) rather more intelligibly, but no more convincingly, maintains that the cosender is not a coauthor. Lietzmann (1949, 4) gratuitously transforms the cosender into a collaborator whose contribution to the letter was at most to help Paul remember things. For Klauck (1987, 17) Sosthenes is mentioned simply to indicate his agreement with the contents of the letter. Fee (1987, 30–31) agrees that "Sosthenes seems to have had nothing to do with the letter as such" but cautiously notes that multiple authorship is such a rare phenomenon in antiquity that "one cannot be certain what to make of it" in the case of the Pauline letters.

This brief survey makes it clear that, instead of responding creatively to the polarity, commentators have simply denied the tension by arbitrarily suppressing one of the contradictory elements. To the best of my knowledge, no one has attempted to determine what contribution Sosthenes might have made to the letter.

Even a superficial reading of 1 Corinthians reveals that a reference to Sosthenes is not implied in every instance of the first person plural. It is equally obvious, however, that the meaning of "we" is not so univocal as positively to exclude Sosthenes in every case. The problem is to determine the various senses in which it is used, and then to decide if any particular category is appropriate to coauthorship.

The most limited uses of the first person plural appear in 8:8, where it is spoken by the strong in their debate with the weak regarding the legitimacy of food offered to idols (Murphy-O'Connor 1979; Fee 1987, 383; NRSV), and in 12:23-24, where it articulates normal human pudency.

The most extensive use of "we" and "our" is found in those passages where Paul affirms something that he has in common, not only with the Corinthians, but with all believers. Baptism (8:6; 12:13) implies commitment to Christ (5:7; 15:3). Negatively this means the rejection of idols (8:1, 4) and positively it implies the choice of a particular lifestyle (5:8; 10:6-11, 22; 11:31-32) whose difficulty is rooted in the weakness of the human condition (13:9, 12; 15:49). Believers are strengthened by the Eucharist (10:16-17) and, though now only on the way to salvation (1:18), can look forward to ultimate victory (6:3, 14; 9:25; 15:51b, 52, 57).

There are three types of more specific usage of the first person plural. Paul and the Corinthians have a relationship to Apollos (16:12), but in a number of passages "we" designates only those two who planted and watered the community at Corinth (3:9; 4:1, 6-13). Paul also uses "we" to associate himself with Barnabas (9:4-6, 10-14) because they shared the same attitude to financial support. Finally, the privilege of having seen the Risen Lord places Paul among those who bear witness to the resurrection (15:11-19).

The most difficult instances of the first person plural to classify are those in 1:18-31 and 2:6-16. The commentators who take up the challenge are few and far between. C. K. Barrett (1968, 54) ignores the problem in 2:6-16 and without explanation interprets 1:23 as "we Christians preach" (as does Merklein 1992, 188). Fee (1987, 75 n. 34), on the other hand, remarks apropos of this latter text, "how natural it is for Paul to slip into this usage; note also that it tends to happen in such places as this, where Paul would be concerned to imply that such preaching is not unique to himself." The contradiction betrays the speculative character of both hypotheses. Moreover, the nature of Paul's evocation of all believers through the use of "we" (see above) is markedly different to what appears here, and there is reason to think that Paul was in fact unique in his consistent stress on the brutal modality of Christ's death.[11] Following Lietzmann (1949, 11), Fee (1987, 101 n. 13) treats the first person plural in 2:6-16 as representing Paul's "common editorial 'we,' " and thus equivalent to "I," as his exegesis makes clear. However common it might be elsewhere (the cautionary remarks of Roller [1933, 169] should be noted), this literary device is unattested for this period in Paul's career; it cannot be simply postulated as if it were a well-documented, habitual technique of the apostle.

Typical of a certain type of solution is E. E. Ellis' suggestion (1978, 26) that "we" appears in 2:6-16 because it was originally a text "created within a (Pauline) group of pneumatics prior to its use in 1 Corinthians 2." By "we," it is claimed, the spirit-people referred to themselves; hence the hiatus when one tries to understand it of Paul. The most radical version of this approach is the claim that 2:6-16 represents the views of the spirit-people at Corinth which they inserted when 1 Corinthians was being compiled (Widman 1979). I have elsewhere indicated (1986, 81-84) why this latter hypothesis is unacceptable. There is some truth in Ellis' position, but not in the sense that he intends. Paul does here reproduce the theology of his opponents, the spirit-people, but only in order to transform and ridicule it (Fee 1987, 100). When viewed in this perspective the "we" remains unexplained. Nonetheless, both authors put us on the right track by their perception of a certain distance between the apostle and the text.

I once suggested that by "we" in 2:6-16 Paul intended to associate himself with Apollos, who had been set over against him by those who considered themselves the spiritual elite of the Corinthian Church (1986, 82). Now I am not at all sure that this is correct. It is not recommended by the context. Apollos had been mentioned previously (1:12), but only as one in a list. Moreover,

[11]Whereas the creed merely mentions the death of Christ (1 Cor 15:3), Paul preaches "Christ crucified" (1 Cor 1:17, 23; 2:2, etc.). All the traditional material in the Pauline letters focuses only on the fact of Jesus' death, without specifying the way in which it came about, but Paul adds "death on a cross" (Phil 2:8) and "by the blood of his cross" (Col 1:20) to preexistent hymns. See my "Another Jesus (2 Cor 11:4)," *RB* 97 (1992) 238-51.

the concern of 2:6-16 is to knock the spirit-people off balance by mocking their intellectual pretensions. Attention is focused on the game of giving new values to their cherished concepts. Their understanding of Paul's relationship to Apollos is dealt with only in 3:5. Since none of the solutions proposed to explain the presence of "we" in 1:18-31 and 2:6-16 carry conviction, it is perhaps time to envisage seriously the possibility that the first person plural in these passages indicates a contribution of Sosthenes to the formulation of 1 Corinthians.

The continuous cross-references in the commentaries make it unnecessary to demonstrate how closely interrelated are these two passages. Not only do they focus on the same problem (the misuse of wisdom speculation by the spirit-people at Corinth), but, as Ellis (1978, 155–56, 213–14) has shown, they exhibit the same basic three-part structure of (1) theme and initial Old Testament texts, (2) exposition linked to the initial and final texts by catchwords, and (3) final Old Testament text.[12] This precise pattern is reproduced nowhere else in the Pauline letters. It is as specific to 1 Corinthians as the presence of Sosthenes in the address.

The possibility that Sosthenes had a hand in the formulation of 1:18-31 and 2:6-16 is moved towards the level of probability by the relationship of these passages to the subsequent paragraph in each case, namely 2:1-5 and 3:1-4 respectively. In 1:18-31 and 2:6-16 we have theoretical arguments on the level of principle, whereas 2:1-5 and 3:1-4 are eminently practical in their stress on the necessity of judging by results, not by intentions. These latter betray the quintessential Paul, whose pragmatism was one of the factors which alienated the spirit-people; his lack of sympathy with their legitimate desire for a speculative theology was why they turned to Apollos (Merklein 1992, 134–39). The irritation perceptible in the emphatic *kago* which introduces both 2:1-5 and 3:1-4[13]—a further unique feature insofar as in only these two instances

[12]The validity of the observation is not compromised by the highly debatable hypotheses which Ellis has built upon it, namely, that 1:18-31 and 2:6-16 were originally independent midrashim. See Fee (1987, 101 n. 13) and Merklein (1992, 175).

[13]This is well brought out by the *Bible de Jérusalem* which uses "Pour moi" in both cases. English versions are neither as perceptive nor consistent

in the Pauline epistles does it begin a new paragraph—suggests that Paul had become impatient with the somewhat diffuse sophistication of 1:18-31 and 2:6-16 and intervened to state his basic position with brutal simplicity. It is improbable that this situation would have arisen were Paul the sole author of 1:18-31 and 2:6-16. It seems much more likely that, when it came to dealing with the divisive influence of the spirit-people, Paul took the advice of a collaborator as regards form and content, which gave the latter the status of a coauthor, but also insisted on making his point in his own way.

Obviously this argument would be greatly strengthened if it were certain that the Sosthenes named in the address was the erstwhile *archisynagogos*, "synagogue benefactor," of Corinth (Acts 18:17). Not only would he then have had firsthand information on the affairs of the community, but his role in the synagogue would have given him some familiarity with the exposition and use of Scripture. Unfortunately, we can be sure only that the Sosthenes of the letter was known to its recipients (Fee 1987, 31; Merklein 1992, 68). It is curious, nonetheless, that Paul invokes his aid only with regard to the divisions within the community. It would seem that, while Chloe's people reported various parties (1:11-12), Sosthenes was the one to single out the spirit-people as the real danger, and to suggest a way in which they might be neutralized. His contribution was not required on the practical issues which occupy the rest of 1 Corinthians.

Second Corinthians

The interplay of "I" and "we" in 2 Corinthians has received much more attention than that in 1 Corinthians. Regrettably, the only result is a greater variety of implausible explanations.

At one extreme we encounter a flat refusal to admit the possibility of coauthorship "because one is conscious all the while that Paul is the author" (Furnish 1984, 104; similarly Allo 1956, 2). Despite the subjectivity of this conviction there is a laudable concern to justify the presence of Timothy in the address. He is men-

---

but the NAB translates 2:1 by "As for myself," and the RSV has "But I" in 3:1.

tioned, we are told, (1) to demonstrate his approval of the contents (Allo 1956, 2), (2) to show his continuing concern for the Corinthians (Furnish 1984, 104), (3) to manifest that he still had Paul's support and so rehabilitate him in the eyes of the Corinthians (Martin 1986, 2), and (4) to fulfil the legal requirement of Deuteronomy 19:15 that all testimony be sustained by at least two witnesses (Furnish 1984, 104). The absence of contemporary epistolary parallels condemn all these hypotheses (note particularly Taatz for (4)).

Others avoid the issue of coauthorship and reduce the person of Timothy to insignificance by highlighting the polyvalence of the first person plural in 2 Corinthians. Windisch (1924, 2) admits that it can include Timothy, for example, when he and Paul share a common experience or when they are united against the Corinthians, but most often, he maintains, it means "we apostles/missionaries" or "we Christians." This singleminded concern with the inclusive versus exclusive use of the first person plural dominates the rather confused investigations of Prümm (1960, 31–35) and Baumert (1973, 23–36). Their approach was refined and clarified by Carrez, who distinguishes four uses of "we" in 2 Corinthians (1) we = you, the community; (2) we = collaborators of Paul who were not apostles; (3) we = the apostles; and (4) we = I (i.e., the epistolary plural). This classification was adopted without modification by Klauck (1986, 12) who, nonetheless, draws attention (1986, 17) to the fact that it is very difficult to find unambiguous examples of (3). He rightly rejects the claim of Carrez to find this sense in 10:4-8, 12-13—if anything they belong to (4)—but his own proposal of 1:24 or 5:18, 20 is equally unconvincing. This point is important because, if sense (3) is excluded, this variety of usage of the first person plural is in no way opposed to coauthorship. Klauck, curiously, claims that Timothy shared responsibility for the content of 2 Corinthians without being in any way englobed in the first personal plural! (1986, 17).

At the other extreme are those who wholeheartedly embrace coauthorship. Even though he denies it to Sosthenes in 1 Corinthians, Fee (1987, 30) is prepared to accord a role in the actual writing of 2 Corinthians to Timothy, but does not go into detail. Bultmann (1976, 24) takes it for granted that Timothy is the coauthor, and, as so often exegetically, asks the critical question (to which he does not attempt an answer): what is the extent of his contribution? Attempts to respond to this question by Prior (1989, 42 n. 19) and Richards (1991, 155–57) break down because they fail to discern any pattern in the use of "we" and "I." The latter, nonetheless, makes a contribution by highlighting a fundamental statistic derived (with corrections) from Carrez's tabulation of the use of the first person singular and plural in 2 Corinthians:

	I	*We*
2 Cor 1–9	81 (26 percent)	225 (74 percent)
2 Cor 10–13	147 (74 percent)	51 (26 percent)

Not only does this table graphically confirm the difference between the two letters, but it reveals that the "I/we" problem in 2 Cor 1–9 is the opposite of that in 1 Corinthians. The latter is essentially an "I-letter" in which it is necessary to explain the plurals, whereas 2 Corinthians 1–9 is essentially a "We-letter" in which it is the singulars that require explanation. In other words, given the address there is a *prima facie* case that 2 Corinthians 1–9 is a joint letter into which one of the coauthors occasionally erupts.[14]

Windisch (1924, 33) almost had the solution within his grasp by noting the alternation of "we" and "I" passages, but failed because he permitted himself to be side-tracked into nonessentials. Only when the broad pattern is perceived can the details be properly understood. In the following table the number in square brackets after a reference indicates the number of exceptions (i.e., "I" in "we" sections and vice versa):

Section	*We*	*I*
A	1:3–14	
B		1:15–17
C	1:18–22	
D		1:23–2:13 [1]

[14]Since 2 Cor is made up of two letters there is a theoretical doubt as to which of them the address belongs. The issue is discussed by Furnish (1984, 101–2) who rightly concludes that it belongs to 2 Cor 1–9.

Section	*We*	*I*
E	2:14–7:2 [2]	
F		7:3-12 [1]
G	7:13–8:7 [3]	
H		8:8-15
J	8:16-24 [1]	
K		9:1-15 [1]

The regularity of the pattern is noteworthy. Five "we" sections alternate with the same number of "I" sections. The apparent equality evaporates, and the disproportion highlighted by Carrez and Richards is confirmed, when the sections are roughly quantified by the number of verses. The "we" sections total 122 verses (72 percent) whereas the "I" sections amount to only 47 verses (28 percent). Moreover, the latter focus on only two issues, the "intermediate visit" and the collection for the poor of Jerusalem.

THE "I" SECTIONS

Sections B, D, and F deal with the consequences of the "intermediate visit" in which Timothy was not involved; he had been sent to Macedonia (Acts 19:22) when Paul was forced to change his plans (cf. 1 Cor 16:5). In itself this is sufficient to identify the first person singular, which in theory could evoke either Paul or Timothy, as referring to the former. The letter written in tears (2:4) was as deeply personal as Paul's joy at the effect it produced (7:7). In these sections, therefore, a shift from the plural to the singular is not only appropriate but necessary.

The occasional shift back to the plural is easily explained. Timothy had exercised an official mission to Corinth (1:24; cf. 1 Cor 4:17; 16:10-11), and he had been with Paul in Macedonia (Acts 19:22) when Titus finally arrived from Corinth; thus the shift into the plural in 7:5 is just as natural as the transition back, "he told us of your longing, your mourning, your zeal for me, so that I rejoiced still more" (7:7).

Sections H and K concern the collection. Paul intervenes in H (8:8-15) to prevent a misunderstanding of the *hina* clause in 8:7. Its imperatival force (BDF §387[3]; Furnish 1984, 403) reflects Paul and Timothy's concern that the Corinthians should actually do something for the poor of Jerusalem, but it was against the former's principles to coerce a moral decision (Phlm 8, 14; 2 Cor 9:7). Hence it is Paul who breaks in with "I say this not as a command" (cf. 1 Cor 7:6), and continues with a Christological reference and a *quid pro quo* argument which he has already used in financial matters in 1 Corinthians 9:11.

Section K (9:1-15) is the conclusion of the letter, and is a highly personal appeal which shades into a profound theological argument. The striking parallel with Galatians 6:11-18 identifies it as a personal postscript, which is as much a feature of Paul's epistolary technique as it was of those of his contemporaries (Richards 1991, 80-90, 176-82). In order to authenticate a letter written by a secretary, the author personally had to write the last paragraph. In the case of a joint letter, a choice had to be made, and the leader was the obvious candidate. Thus we must assume that the "I" here refers to Paul (cf. 2 Thess 3:17-18). This convention explains not only the shift from the plural to the singular but also the duality of chapters 8 and 9. It was inevitable that Paul should personalize the joint appeal for the poor (Gal 2:10).

Somewhat surprisingly the first person plural surfaces in 9:4b ("lest we be humiliated"), but presumably Timothy had done his share of boasting about the Corinthians in order to encourage the Macedonians to be generous.

THE "WE" SECTIONS

As noted earlier, the different senses which can and have been assigned to the first person plural do not of themselves exclude Timothy as coauthor. Just as an individual can identify with a group of ministers or a community or believers in general, so too can a couple. A more serious obstacle to granting Timothy a substantial role in the composition of the letter is perhaps unconscious. The Church's recognition of the importance of Paul's role in the establishment of Christianity encourages the belief that Paul thought of himself as unique and that, in consequence, the long section on the apostolate (2:14–7:2) must be understood as if Paul was speaking above all of himself (Baumert 1973, 29, 36; Klauck 1986, 12). The validity of this assumption needs to be assessed. Did Paul think of himself as unique and, if so, in what sense?

As the last beneficiary of a post-paschal appearance (1 Cor 15:8) Paul had seen the Lord (1 Cor 9:1). No others in the Diaspora could make a similar claim, but it became important to stress this point only after he had broken with the Church of Antioch. As their emissary (Acts 13:2-3) he had no need to identify himself. Thus he presents himself without qualification in 1 and 2 Thessalonians. Subsequently, having lost that legitimizing base, he was obliged to insist on the divine initiative in his commission, and to identify himself as "an apostle of Christ Jesus by the will of God" (1 Cor 1:1 and all subsequent letters with the exception of Phil and Phlm). Paul was also conscious that he had an authority equal to that of Peter and James, even though he had never known the earthly Jesus (Gal 2:1-14). Thus, in terms of the origin of his ministry and its resultant status, there was no parallel between Paul and even his closest collaborators. This is borne out by the way he speaks of them. He only once brackets himself and Timothy together and then it is as "slaves of Christ Jesus" (Phil 1:1), not as recipients of a direct divine mandate.

On the practical level of day-to-day ministry, however, there was no essential difference between Paul and the many others who founded and nurtured new churches. They all acted as channels of grace which brought into being a new creation. Differences of theology and approach, and even motive, were accidental, as Paul himself recognized (Phil 1:15-18). Thus there is nothing in 2:14–7:4 which is limited to Paul. It is a vision of ministry which he hoped would inspire and be adopted by all, and in particular by his opponents at Corinth. There can be little doubt that Timothy modelled his pastoral practice on that of Paul and, once this is recognized, there can be no objection to finding him consciously and deliberately reflected in the first person plurals of 2 Corinthians. Precise positive evidence of his contribution might be difficult to determine, but by comparison with the inept approach of 1 Corinthians, the change in tone and tactics in dealing with the problem of the spirit-people is remarkable (Murphy-O'Connor 1986b), and input on the part of Timothy is the simplest explanation for the refinement of Paul's approach.

We must now look at the occasional presence of the first person singular in the "we" sections. They are so characteristic of

Paul's temperament that, far from undermining the coauthorship hypothesis, they rather support it.

The two interjections in section E are brief and bitter: "I hope that it is known also to your consciences" (5:11) and "I speak as to children" (6:13).[15] They betray the impatience of an emotional Paul with the working out of a delicate and complex argument. The same phenomenon has already been noted in 1 Corinthians 2:1-5 and 3:1-4.

The three interventions in section G and the one in section J are of a different type. Paul's relief and happiness at the reconciliation which he believes to have been effected by Titus is irrepressible and breaks out at 7:14 and 16 in effusive compliments to the Corinthians. Timothy, I suspect, was less sanguine. The same enthusiasm, but this time inspired by the the Macedonians, bubbles up in "I swear, even beyond what they were able" (8:3). At this point Paul was prepared to love the whole world. His gratitude to Titus demands something more than the official compliments of 8:6 and 8:16-17 and erupts in the superfluous "As for Titus he is my partner and co-worker in your service" (8:23a), which necessitates a further gracious reference to those accompanying him (8:23b).

2 CORINTHIANS 10–13

The question of coauthorship does not arise for letters whose address does not mention multiple senders. The original address of 2 Cor 10–13 was abandoned when it was combined with 2 Cor 1–9, and thus we can never know whether it was a joint or individual letter. The heightened feeling and intensely personal tone would suggest the latter. Confirmation, however, cannot be claimed from the statistics cited above which reveal the predominance of the first person singular because this is also the case in 1 Corinthians where, nonetheless, the contributions of a coauthor were detected.

The only passage where the hand of a coauthor might possibly be detected is 10:12-18. As many commentators have seen, this

[15]The closest parallel to 6:13 is 1 Cor 3:1, which also lacks the affectionate overtones of 1 Cor 1:14; Gal 4:19; and 1 Thess 2:7-8.

block of material is a neatly rounded whole inspired by the reference to "work" in the epistolary plural in 10:11 (Plummer 1915, 285; Windisch 1924, 307; Bultmann 1976, 193; Martin 1986, 314; Klauck 1986, 80; Wolff 1989, 203). In opposition to the other instances of the first person plural in chapters 10–13, the use of "we" is consistent throughout; the only comparable section, 13:4-9, is spoiled by the appearance of the first person singular in 13:6. Moreover, it closes with precisely the same free adaptation of the LXX version of Jeremiah 9:24 found in 1 Corinthians 1:31, which is the conclusion of the coauthored section 1 Corinthians 1:18-31. Finally, the paradoxical twist of the indirect argument is reminiscent of the spirit behind 1 Corinthians 2:6-16 (Windisch 1924, 307). The value of these arguments, however, is negated by the improbability of their conclusion, for they point, not to Timothy as coauthor, but to Sosthenes. It seems more likely, therefore, that in 10:12-18 Paul is speaking of the missionary strategy of his team, which he of course determined.

Other Letters

Thus far we have seen that Silvanus and Timothy, Sosthenes, and Timothy made substantial contributions to 1 and 2 Thessalonians, 1 Corinthians and 2 Corinthians 1–9 respectively, even though the degree of their involvement varied, being greatest in the Thessalonian letters and least in 1 Corinthians.

These conclusions would appear to be endangered by the fact that the assumption that the mention of cosenders implies coauthors is not verified for Galatians, Philippians, and Philemon. On the contrary, the challenge of these letters is to discover why Paul listed cosenders who did not function as coauthors.

The formulation of the address in Galatians is not intended to imply coauthorship; the unspecified brethren are mentioned in order to evoke the solidarity of the Pauline Church against the Judaizers (Schlier 1962, 28–29). An instructive parallel is furnished by an early Christian letter: "Polycarp and the presbyters with him to the church of God sojourning at Philippi." There is no doubt here that the letter was written by Polycarp personally but his motive in associating his clergy with him in the address was to underline that he was not writing as a private individual.

The case of Philippians is more complicated because, as I have noted above, it is a combination of three epistles (*Letter A*: 1:3–3:1 and 4:2-9; *Letter B:* 3:2-4:1; *Letter C*: 4:10-20) and it is uncertain to which, if any, of these the address naming Timothy as cosender belonged (1:1). Letters A and C use the first person singular exclusively, the one exception being "our God" in 4:20. Letter B is a different matter. "I" predominates but "we" appears in six instances. In 3:3, 15, 16, 20, 21 the meaning is clearly "we believers." In the one remaining instance (3:17) the shift from singular to plural and back indicates that the "we" is epistolary.

Paul associates himself with Timothy in the address of Philemon, which is directed to a group of three, Philemon, Apphia, and Archippus. Yet the reality of the letter is summed up in *egrapsa soi,* "I wrote to thee" (v. 21). It is a message from one individual to another. The rare plurals are perfunctory (vv. 2, 3, 22, 25) and certainly do not evoke a coauthor. Since the letter is addressed to three individuals, one might think of the letters of Cicero to his wife and Tiro, were it not for the presence of "and to the church in your house" (1:2). These words transfer the letter from the private to the public sector and force us to ask: Why did Paul give a purely personal entreaty the character of an official letter? We might speculate that it was to ensure that it was read in the presence of all the members of the Church, and thereby to bring not so subtle pressure on the owner of Onesimus to accede to Paul's request for his liberation.

The body of Colossians (2:6–4:2) is devoid of either "I" or "we." These appear only at the beginning and end of the letter. The fact that the thanksgiving (1:3-23a) is in the first person plural ranges this epistle with 1 and 2 Thessalonians and 2 Corinthians 1–9. The intrusive character of the "I" section (1:23b-2:5) is highlighted by the abrupt "I, Paul" with which it begins. This section is a highly personal reflection on his sufferings and mission which, after the lapidary traditional statement of the meaning of ministry in the first person plural (1:28), continues with insistence on the depth of his concern for believers at Colossae and Laodicea. In the conclusion of the letter the plural appears only at 4:3a, where the Colossians are requested to pray for "us," and in 4:8, where Tychicus is to report on "how we are." The rest is in the first person singular and focuses on Paul's imprisonment and on those who have remained loyal to him. In sum, therefore, Colossians is a "we" letter into which Paul has interjected personal reflections. There is no valid reason to deny that Timothy made a substantive contribution to its composition.

Coauthorship in Practice

How did coauthorship work in practice? In the light of what Pliny the Younger has said about his working habits (*Letters* 9:36 quoted p. 10 above), we might reasonably assume that, whereas Pliny communed with himself, Paul consulted his companions and, as the leader, did the actual dictation. Within this broad framework, however, circumstances influenced the exact procedure in each letter.

At the time of composition of 1 and 2 Thessalonians, Paul was still a neophyte both as a leader and a writer. The committee of three produced the letters, and Paul kept his personal comments to the minimum. As the one dictating, however, he could interject without difficulty.

The circumstances of 1 Corinthians were very different. Not only was Paul much more experienced, but he was consulted officially by the Church of Corinth. The delegation (16:17) brought a letter (7:1) to which he was expected to respond. His decision to involve a coauthor can only have been motivated by his need for local knowledge to deal with certain problematic situations which were not alluded to in the letter but which were reported by Chloe's people (1:11). Working with Sosthenes, however, proved less satisfactory than anticipated; he appears to have been one of those people who are briskly insightful in conversation but complicated and overly subtle in formulating a text. Paul gave him two chances and then in irritation abandoned him.

The effect of 1 Corinthians at Corinth did not conform to Paul's expectations; it served only to intensify the alienation of the spirit-people. The apostle's relations with Corinth deteriorated further during the "intermediate visit," and, once dispatched, the "severe letter" (2 Cor 2:4) occasioned him profound anxiety (2 Cor 7:8). Should he have sent it in anger? Would its harsh language produce the desired effect? It is not at all surprising, therefore, that he should have invoked the aid of Timothy in the delicate task of composing 2 Cor 1–9. They worked consistently and well together, notably in the major section on the apostolate (2:14–7:2), but the nature of some of the material forced Paul to be highly personal. Such interventions tended to run on a little too long. Each time this happened, however, Timothy was able to get Paul back to the cooperative task which eventually produced the most extraordinary letter in the New Testament.

Paul again had recourse to Timothy's skills only when he had to deal with the novel form of opposition which arose at Colossae.

A PAULINE STYLE?

An important implication of the previous two sections is that the argument from style, which has been used to determine the authenticity and inauthenticity of certain letters, can no longer be considered valid.

While it is unlikely that the Apostle would be party to the deception involved in commissioning anyone to write a letter in his name, there can be little doubt that in any of the major cities from which Paul wrote (Corinth, Ephesus, Philippi, Thessalonica) a variety of stenographic help was available to assist him in recording his letters. If there was no one to take speed dictation, he simply had to slow to the pace of whoever was prepared to serve him.

Which system he used is impossible to determine with any certitude. According to Richards, the only epistle likely to have been written down at the speed of ordinary speech is Romans, "The letter that contains the strongest oral features, that contains such a high frequency of oratorical rhetoric, that perhaps has the strongest possibility of being all or partly *ipsissima verba Pauli viva voce*" (1991, 171; cf. Roller 1933, 8–14). On much the same grounds, in my view, an identical claim can be made for 2 Corinthians 10–13.

In opposition to these two highly individual letters stand 1 and 2 Thessalonians, 1 Corinthians, 2 Corinthians 1–9, and Colossians, in which the presence of one or more coauthors has been detected. If the quality of secretarial help affected Paul's presentation, coauthors had an even greater impact. The input of others would not only have modified Paul's dictation technique, but might also have imposed different vocabulary and verbal patterns.

Our inability to determine in precise detail the contribution of a coauthor, to set out the extent of secretarial involvement, and to fix the number of secretaries employed makes it impossible to define Paul's style in such a way as to permit the detection of significant variations from that norm. This conclusion is confirmed by recent stylistic studies.

Early stylistic analyses of the epistles rarely amounted to anything more than the listing of a few generic indicators (e.g., the number of hapaxlegomena) in order to confirm conventional impressions. Such crudity has given place to sophisticated statistical analyses. The most important recent contributions are Anthony Kenny's *A Stylometric Study of the New Testament* (Oxford: Clarendon, 1986) and Kenneth J. Neumann's *The Authenticity of the Pauline Epistles in the Light of Stylostatistical Analysis* (SBLDS 120; Atlanta: Scholars Press, 1990). Both studies highlight their own lack of precision and, somewhat surprisingly in view of the current consensus, conclude that Ephesians, Colossians, and 2 Thessalonians have as much in common with Romans, Galatians, and 1 and 2 Corinthians as these latter have with each other. There is little doubt that a single mind lies behind most of the Pauline corpus. But the differences, even between letters universally accepted as authentic, are far from negligible, and demand an explanation. Of the possible explanations a variety of secretaries and coauthors is the simplest (Prior 1989, 49; Richards 1991, 186).

NOTE-TAKERS AND CHURCH TRADITION

The role of the recording secretary with respect to archival material and incoming data has been noted above (p. 13). It is to the great credit of Richards (1991, 158–68) that he has drawn attention to the possible relevance of such practice for Paul's career.

Even though Paul claimed regarding his gospel that "I did not receive it from anyone, nor was I taught it" (Gal 1:12), he could not have escaped the influence of the communities in which he lived, notably Damascus and Antioch. In fact, his letters betray indisputable dependence on the dogmatic and liturgical tradition of the early Church (Hunter 1961; Guthrie 1966, 270–73; Barth 1984; Ellis 1986). His references to handing on what he had himself received (1 Cor 11:23; 15:3) are confirmed by the citation of credal formulae (1 Cor 15:3-5; Rom 1:3-4; 4:25; 8:34; 10:8-9; 1 Thess 1:10; Gal 1:3-4), liturgical hymns (Phil 2:6-11; Col 1:15-20; 1 Tim 3:16; Eph 5:14), the words of institution of the Eucharist (1 Cor 11:23-25), and catechetical material (1 Thess 4:1-12; Gal 5:19-21).

Paul may have had a particularly retentive memory, but it would have been more in keeping with the ethos of his age to have noted, either personally or by a secretary, such items as he felt might be useful in his oral instruction and written communication. When a prisoner he wrote to Timothy, "When you come, bring the cloak that I left with Carpus at Troas, also the books and above all the notebooks [*kai ta biblia, malista tas membranas*]" (2 Tim 4:13).[16] *Membrana* was borrowed from Latin, and in the first century designated parchment notebooks, the small codices which had replaced wooden waxed tablets (Roberts and Skeat 1983, 15–23). The point is perfectly illustrated by Martial's epigram,

Parchment Tablets
Imagine these tablets are waxen, although they are called parchment. You will rub out as often as you wish to write afresh (*Epigrams* 14:7; Ker).[17]

Ignorance of this text led to the translation of *membranai* in 2 Timothy 4:13 by the generic "parchments" (e.g., RSV, JB, NAB), which has given rise to a multitude of opinions regarding Paul's meaning (Spicq 1969, 815–16). Most are excluded by the specific meaning "notebooks," which suggests that Paul had in mind the

---

[16]Skeat has argued that *biblia* and *membranai* refer to the same reality because *malista* in Gal 6:10 and 1 Tim 4:10 has a restrictive function. *Malista,* however, has a distinguishing function in Phil 4:22; Phlm 16; 1 Tim 5:8, 17; Titus 1:10.

[17]The title translates *Pugillares Membranei,* which is explained as "parchments of a size to be held in one's fist" (BAGD s.v. *membrana,* 502a).

bound sheets of parchment on which he had recorded traditional items which impressed him, or noted ideas for sermons, or roughed out approaches he felt might be effective with different communities whose difficulties had been reported to him.

There is also the distinct possibility that such notebooks contained archival material, namely, copies of the letters which Paul had sent to the Churches for which he was responsible. As we have seen above (p. 12), it was normal practice to retain copies of letters dispatched. This is developed by Richards (1991, 165 n. 169) into the proposal that "the first collection of Paul's letters were in codex form and arose from Paul's personal copies and *not* from collecting the letters from various recipients. . . . Two implications arise from such a theory: (1) The so-called lost letters were not copied before dispatching, perhaps due to haste, and not letters which were somehow misplaced. (2) Such a collection might easily fall into Luke's hands at the death of Paul (2 Tim 4:11)'' (see also Archer 1951–52, 297). The simplicity of this hypothesis contributes to its attractiveness, but its evaluation must be reserved to the discussion of the formation of the Pauline canon (p. 118).

SENDING A LETTER

The emperor Augustus (27 B.C.–A.D. 14) was the first to establish a regular postal service in the west. According to Suetonius (ca. A.D. 68–ca. 140):

> To enable what was going on in each of the provinces to be reported and known more speedily and promptly [in Rome], he at first stationed young men along the military roads and afterwards post-chaises. The latter has seemed the more convenient arrangement, since the same men who bring the dispatches from any place can, if occasion demands, be questioned as well (*Augustus* 49; Rolfe).

In other words, he first instituted a relay system, in which dispatches were passed from hand to hand along a series of messengers, but later set up stations offering a change of horses, which permitted messengers to go right through at an average speed of fifty miles a day. Our word *post* derives from *positus*, the Latin name for such "fixed" stations (White 1986, 214).

Even though the system was certainly abused in particular instances, the imperial mail carried only official correspondence. Private individuals had to make their own arrangements. The options open to them depended on their means (Westermann 1928). Wealthy people could employ slaves or freedmen as letter-carriers, as we gather from Cicero's reply to Papirius Paetus:

> There are two letters of yours which I shall answer—one which I received four days ago from Zethus, the other which was brought me by your letter-carrier Phileros (*Fam* 9:15.1; Williams).

Atticus could afford to do likewise. Cicero narrates a coincidence:

> I had just taken the turn off the road to Antium on to the Appian Way at the Three Taverns on the very day of the Cerealia, when my friend Curio met me fresh from Rome: and at the very same moment your man with a letter (*Att* 2:12.2; Winstedt).

For longer distances it was possible for such people to combine. Thus when Julius Caesar was campaigning in Gaul, his agent Gaius Oppius arranged for letters to be sent on a regular basis to him and his officers, one of whom was Cicero's brother. Cicero responded to one of the latter's complaints:

> I come now to your letters. which I received in several packets when I was at Aprinum. In fact, three were delivered to me in one day, and apparently dispatched by you at the same time, one of them of considerable length, in which the first thing you noticed was that my letter to you bore an earlier date than that to Caesar. That is what Oppius occasionally cannot help doing. I mean that, when he has decided to send letter-carriers and has received a letter from me, something unexpected occurs to hinder him, and he is unavoidably later than he intended in sending the carriers; while I, when once the letter has been handed to him, do not trouble about having the date altered (*QFr* 3:1.8; Williams).

Even among the privileged, this type of direct, organized service was rare. In the vast majority of cases, the sending of a letter depended on the availability of a traveller going in the right direction. In his haste to reply to Atticus, Cicero wrote:

> I write this on the day of the Cerealia at four o'clock, as soon as I read yours, but I am thinking of giving it to the first person I meet tomorrow (*Att* 2:12.4; Winstedt).

He was not very fortunate in his choice, because he wrote to Atticus on 23 April, "What a shame! The letter I wrote on the spur of the moment at the Three Taverns in answer to your delightful notes never reached you!" (*Att* 2:13.1; Winstedt).

A letter could be lost accidentally (*Att* 2:8.1). The bearer could decide not to hurry—one slave held a letter for forty days before moving (*Fam* 8:12.4)—or forget the commission completely. If someone of Cicero's stature had problems, it takes little imagination to understand the plight of the poor, who paid in the hope that the donkey or camel drivers (see the letter of Indike, p. 99 below), who carried their letters, were honest. Not all were, and those deceived had no recourse. Sabinianus expresses his gratitude for the help given his sister by Apollinarius. Despite appearances, he claims, it is not the first time. "I wrote to you often, and the negligence of those who carry [the letters] has accused us falsely as negligent" (*PMich* VIII, 499; White, 1986, 183). Trustworthiness took on another dimension when the contents of the letter were confidential; nosey bearers were easily tempted to lighten the weight of a letter by reading it (*Att* 1:13.1). The only option then was to use someone fully in the confidence of the sender, as Brutus pointed out to Cicero.

> Please write me a reply to this letter at once, and send one of your own men with it, if there is anything somewhat confidential which you think it necessary for me to know (*Fam* 11:20.4; Williams).

Such a bearer, of course, could supplement the contents of the letter by verbal information or by answering questions. In addition to *PLond* 42 (quoted p. 57 below), this point is made explicitly in a letter to Zenon. "The rest please learn from the man who brings you the letter, for he is not a stranger to us" (*PColZen* I, 6; White, 1984, 1732).

Very often the motive for writing a letter was the accidental discovery of someone going to the place with which one wanted to communicate. The young Egyptian soldier Apollinarios wrote to his mother, not because he needed anything, but simply because he had an opportunity which might not come again quickly. "When I found someone who was journeying to you from Cyrene, I thought it a necessity to inform you about my welfare" (*PMich* VIII, 490; White 1986, 162).

It is not improbable that the availability of messengers was one of the principal criteria used by Paul in the selection of his missionary centers. Both Corinth and Ephesus had excellent communications with all points of the compass, since people from virtually all countries passed through their gates "as traders or pilgrims or envoys or passing travellers" (Dio Chrysostom, *Discourses,* 37:36).

At the beginning Paul may have had to rely on strangers for the transmission of 1 and 2 Thessalonians, but as the network of his communities grew so did the possibility of using Christians to deliver his letters. Thus the "previous letter" (1 Cor 5:9) may have been brought to Corinth by Chloe's people (1 Cor 1:11) when they went there on business from Ephesus. It is most probable that the delegation (1 Cor 16:17) which brought the letter of the Corinthians to Paul (1 Cor 7:1) also brought back his response, namely, 1 Corinthians. The bearer of the "severe letter" (2 Cor 2:4) was Titus, because Paul was on tenterhooks until he brought back an optimistic report of the positive impact it had on the Corinthians (2 Cor 7:6-13). The same assistant was also the bearer of 2 Corinthians 1–9, because he was going back to Corinth with the responsibility of persuading the Corinthians to contribute generously to the collection for the poor of Jerusalem (2 Cor 8:6).

If Phoebe was going to Rome (Rom 16:1-2) and Epaphras, Tychicus, and Onesimus were travelling to Colossae (Col 1:7; 4:7-9), it would make sense for them to carry Romans and Colossians (and Philemon?) respectively. Both of these deductions are given high probability by the commendation of Phoebe and Epaphras, which was a feature of ancient letters (Richards 1991,

8, 70–71), and by the assertion that supplementary information could be had from Tychicus and Onesimus (cf. above).

It is possible that the crisis letters, Galatians and 2 Corinthians 10–13, were carried back by those who brought the bad news from Galatia and Corinth respectively. This is all the more likely if it were Titus who reported on the situation at Corinth. In the case of Galatia, those who drew Paul's attention to the growing influence of the Judaizers there might not have been Galatians. The blanket condemnation of the community (Gal 1:6) in fact suggests that Paul had no supporters there (contrast 1 Cor 1:12). Thus the informants are likely to have been believers who made a brief stopover there while enroute from Antioch to Ephesus, as Chloe's people had temporarily sojourned in Corinth. In this instance, therefore, Paul had to find a letter-carrier of sufficient authority to ensure that his message to the Galatians was not suppressed.

As a circular letter Ephesians must have had a number of bearers. We do not know how 1 and 2 Timothy and Titus were distributed.

2

Organizing a Letter

The letters which Paul wrote were occasioned by problems in or requests from the communities for which he was responsible. Thus they differ significantly in content. Nonetheless, from the point of view of form, they exhibit a consistent general pattern. The concern of this chapter is to describe this pattern and, by comparing the different letters, to determine the significance of the variations.

This type of synoptic work is most appropriate to the beginning and end of letters, where Paul's formulation is most consistent. It does not work for the body of the letters, as the gallant attempt to create a Pauline synopsis revealed (Francis and Sampley 1975). Thus in this section the focus will be on rhetorical and epistolary criticism. After explaining what is involved, the dangers of misuse of the methods will be highlighted, and their contribution to understanding Paul evaluated.

LETTERS OR EPISTLES?

Are what Paul wrote letters or epistles? The question might now appear meaningless but when it was first asked in 1895 by Adolf Deissmann (1901, 3–59) it sparked a debate which enhanced the understanding of Paul.

As Deissmann used the terms a *letter* was one half of a private conversation, therefore individual and personal in nature; it manifested no concern for literary form and style; it was artless and unpremeditated. An *epistle,* on the contrary, was a conscious work of literature, designed to interest as wide a public as possible now and in the future; it resembled the letter only in its epistolary address (Doty 1969).

The validity of the distinction is guaranteed, for example, by a comparison of the chatty letters of Cicero (106–43 B.C.) to Atticus and the sententious "moral epistles" of Seneca (ca. 5 B.C.–A.D. 65). Typical of the former are opening words such as:

> I must tell you that what I most badly need at the present time is a confidant—someone with whom I could share all that gives me any anxiety, a wise, affectionate friend to whom I could talk without pretence or evasion or concealment (*Att* 1:18; Bailey).

> How you whet my appetite about your talk with Bibulus, your discussion with Ox-Eyes, and that apolaustic dinner party too! So come expecting greedy ears (*Att* 2:14; Bailey).

> I hope I may see the day when I shall thank you for making me go on living. So far I am heartily sorry you did (*Att* 3:3; Bailey).

Seneca often begins with a concrete fact, but this is purely a literary device, an attractive beginning to what immediately becomes a philosophical treatise. Much more congruent with the content of his epistles are openings such as:

> It seems to me erroneous to believe that those who have loyally dedicated themselves to philosophy are stubborn and rebellious, scorners of magistrates or kings or of those who control the administration of public affairs (*Ep* 73; Gummere).

> I had been inclined to spare you, and had omitted any knotty problems that still remained undiscussed; I was satisfied to give you a sort of taste of the views held by the men of our school, who desire to prove that virtue is of itself sufficiently capable of rounding out the happy life (*Ep* 85; Gummere).

> You have been wishing to know my views concerning liberal studies (*Ep* 88; Gummere).

The point of the distinction, as far as Deissmann was concerned, was to force those among his contemporaries, who thought of the New Testament writings as something apart and therefore timeless and rootless, to recognize that what Paul wrote were letters, a medium of genuine communication and part of real life in the mid-first century A.D. Once this had been achieved—and it was—the inadequacy of the formulation of the distinction became apparent. Paul wrote to specific people for a limited purpose. In this respect he wrote letters. Nonetheless they were meant for public consumption (Col 4:16). In this respect they are epistles. Yet they are not in intention similar to the epistles of Seneca or Pliny. Thus today no one uses the terms *letter* and *epistle* to imply Deissmann's distinction; they are employed as synonyms. Nonetheless "real letters" and "apparent letters" remain the basic genre categories.

Paul's letters, although they betray evidence of a solid classical education, cannot be classed with, for example, the letters of Cicero. The latter not only had advanced rhetorical training but continuously honed his skills as a practicing lawyer/administrator and as a versatile writer. Neither do the apostle's letters have anything in common with the banal messages which are the content of the papyri letters. They occupy a middle ground which is very difficult to define (Stowers 1986, 25).

From a number of points of view Paul's use of letters is best paralleled by that of Epicurus (341–270 B.C.; Bailey), who "exhorted, encouraged, gave advice, settled disputes, taught his doctrines, and maintained fellowship through his letters" (Stowers 1986, 40). The radical differences between their respective doctrines (e.g., Epicurus' stress on the detachment of the gods and Paul's conviction that the power and wisdom of God were incarnated in Jesus Christ) necessarily mean that the parallels in content are insignificant (Barclay 1960–61). Moreover, as Stowers (1986, 42) points out, Paul's focus is not on the development of individual character but on building communities in which divine grace becomes active.

Despite the nature of his epistles, Seneca beautifully expressed the fundamental fact that a real letter is essentially a substitute for a personal meeting.

I never receive a letter from you without being in your company forthwith. If the pictures of our absent friends are pleasing to us, though they only refresh the memory and lighten our longing by a solace that is unreal and unsubstantial, how much more pleasant is a letter, which brings us real traces, real evidences, of an absent friend! For that which is sweetest when we meet face to face is afforded by the impress of a friend's hand upon his letter—recognition (*Ep* 40:1; Gummere).

It is not surprising, therefore, that a letter should reproduce the basic characteristics of an encounter in which a greeting and leavetaking bracket an exchange of information. Thus a letter is made up of three parts, the address, the body, and the farewell.

ADDRESS

The standard address used by Paul's contemporaries was brief in the extreme. It is typified by "Claudius Lysias to his Excellency the governor Felix, greeting" (Acts 23:26). The two necessary elements were the names of sender and recipient. The formal greeting—*chairein* in Greek or *salus* in Latin (often abbreviated to the initial letter)—could be omitted (e.g., "Cicero to Trebatius" [*Fam* 7:14-15]). Paul always maintains the tripartite address, which he expands considerably but in a variety of ways.

Sender

The question of multiple senders has already been dealt with (p. 16 above). Here our concern is with the description, if any, appended to the names of the senders. The following list graphically displays the diversity. What light do the different formulations throw on Paul's attitude as he wrote?

> *Rom:*   Paul, a servant of Christ Jesus, called to be an apostle, set apart for the gospel of God, which he promised beforehand through his prophets in the holy scriptures, the gospel concerning his son.

1 Cor: Paul, called to be an apostle of Christ Jesus by the will of God, and Sosthenes the brother.

2 Cor: Paul, as apostle of Christ Jesus by the will of God, and Timothy the brother.

Gal: Paul, an apostle, not from men nor by man but by Jesus Christ and God the father who raised him from the dead, and all the believers with me.

Eph: Paul, an apostle of Christ Jesus by the will of God.

Phil: Paul and Timothy, servants of Christ Jesus.

Col: Paul, an apostle of Christ Jesus by the will of God, and Timothy the brother.

1 Thess: Paul, Silvanus, and Timothy.

2 Thess: Paul, Silvanus, and Timothy.

1 Tim: Paul, an apostle of Christ Jesus according to a command of God our Savior and Christ Jesus our hope.

2 Tim: Paul, an apostle of Christ Jesus by the will of God according to the promise of the life which is in Christ Jesus.

Titus: Paul, a servant of God and an apostle of Jesus Christ [to further] the faith of God's elect and [their] knowledge of the truth which accords with holiness, in hope of eternal life which God, who never lies, promised ages ago and at the proper time manifested in his word through the preaching with which I have been entrusted by command of God our Savior.

Phlm: Paul, a prisoner for Christ Jesus, and Timothy the brother.

In both his earliest letters, 1 and 2 Thessalonians, Paul designates himself by name only. It it difficult to know with precision what his next letter was chronologically, but a case can be made that it was Galatians, followed perhaps a year later by 1 Corinthians. In both of these, the divine character of his commissioning as an apostle is stressed in a rather exaggerated way. Something must have happened to transform the confident silence of the assured (1 and 2 Thess) into the verbosity of the ill at ease (Gal,

1 Cor). Paul's vulnerability is explained if in the interval he had lost his legitimizing base by breaking with those who had commissioned him, and was operating on his own; a situation that left him open to the accusation that he was an unrepresentative maverick.

In the light of the available evidence, the only event to fit this scenario is his break with the church at Antioch. Galatians 2:14-21 makes it clear that he no longer shared its values. If he could no longer be a member of that community, a fortiori he could no longer be its representative to the Gentiles. In order to justify his continuing to be a missionary, therefore, he had to stress what he had felt since the moment of his conversion, namely, that he was commissioned directly by God and Christ (cf. 1 Thess 2:7).

The most elaborate formulation of this theme appears in Galatians 1:1. The basis is the radical antithesis "not by man but by Jesus Christ," which is expanded by the bracketing elements "not from men" and "God the father." Nonetheless it is not a chiasm (against Bligh 1969, 61-62). Paul's opponents in Galatia probably belonged to those of his contemporaries who were commissioned by a community ("from men") represented by an individual ("by a man," e.g., James or Peter). The apostle, on the contrary, insists that he was commissioned by "the man" (cf. Rom 5:15-18), whose unquestionable authority, revealed by his resurrection, comes from the Father of all.

It could be argued that Galatians 1:1 represents Paul's initial reflections on breaking with Antioch and that the briefer formulation in 1 Corinthians 1:1 is derived from it. It is equally, if not more, probable, however, that the formulation in Galatians was inspired by the situation there, because a little later in that letter Paul is forced to insist that "the gospel preached by me is not a human creation [*kata anthrōpon*], for I did not receive it from man [*para anthrōpon*], nor was I taught it, but it came through a revelation of Jesus Christ" (Gal 1:11-12). His encounter with the Risen Lord (1 Cor 9:1; 15:8) forced Paul to reevaluate all his ideas. He found himself obliged to recognize the truth of ideas with which he had previously come into contact, but which he had not learned or studied as he had the Law, namely the messianic nature of Jesus and the relative character of the Law (Murphy-O'Connor 1982, 25-27).

Paul stresses his apostolic authority in every subsequent letter, with the exception of Philippians. Such emphasis was all the more necessary in correspondence with communities which in one way or another questioned Paul's authority, namely Corinth, Galatia, and Colossae.

The form of the letter to the last-mentioned Church determined that of Ephesians, whose principle source is Colossians. In Romans Paul was obliged to introduce himself formally to a Church which did not know him. Thus he prefaces the standard "called to be an apostle" by the honorific "servant of Christ Jesus," which evokes the great servants of God in the Old Testament (Sass 1941; Murphy-O'Connor 1964, 55–59), and offers a brief summary of his gospel.

His inclusion of Timothy within this latter title in Philippians, "servants of Christ Jesus" is unique. Since both were in receipt of financial aid from Philippi (Phil 4:18; 2 Cor 11:9), it was appropriate to highlight the intrinsic dignity of their mission. Paul's silence regarding his apostleship is taken to be a clue that there was no threat to his authority at Philippi. This is confirmed by the contents of Philippians, and in particular by Philemon, where Paul wants to avoid any hint of dominance (vv. 10, 14), and so introduces himself as "a prisoner," the emotional basis of his appeal for the release of Onesimus (v. 9).

Much discussion of 1 and 2 Timothy and Titus has been vitiated by the tendency of scholarship to treat them as integral components of a single entity, the Pastorals. Sound methodology demands that each letter be treated on its merits. Sufficient evidence has now been accumulated to put it beyond question that 2 Timothy is clearly distinguished from 1 Timothy and Titus (Prior 1989; Murphy-O'Connor 1991a).

This separation has the further consequence of removing the standard objections to the authenticity of 2 Timothy. Yet, why should Paul need such elaborate self-identification when writing to his oldest and closest collaborator? No certain answer can be given, but I suspect that it reflects the pride of an old campaigner, a theme which runs through the letter (1:11-12; 4:7-8).

The authenticity of 2 Timothy highlights the inauthenticity of 1 Timothy and Titus. As a personal letter addressed to a single individual, 2 Timothy was the exception to Paul's general rule of only writing to communities. Its existence facilitated in the post-Pauline generation the creation of two pseudepigrapha, 1 Timothy and Titus, which represent attempts to capitalize on the authority of Paul. In such cases it is only to be expected that the source of this authority should be stressed in the formulas identifiying the sender, which are notably more elaborate than those in the authentic letters with the exception of Romans, for which an explanation has already been given.

Recipient

The specification of those to whom the letters are addressed takes various forms. What do they tell us about Paul's relationship with his audience?

Rom: To all those who are in Rome beloved by God, called to be saints.

1 Cor: To the church of God which is at Corinth, to those sanctified in Christ Jesus, called to be saints, together with all those who call on the name of the Lord Jesus Christ in every place, theirs and ours.

2 Cor: To the church of God which is at Corinth together with all the saints who are in the whole of Achaia.

Gal: To the assemblies of Galatia.

Eph: To the saints and faithful ones in Christ Jesus.

Phil: To all the saints in Christ Jesus who are at Philippi together with the supervisors and helpers.

Col: To the saints and faithful believers in Christ at Colossae.

1 Thess: To the assembly of the Thessalonians in God the Father and the Lord Jesus Christ.

2 Thess: To the assembly of the Thessalonians in God our Father and the Lord Jesus Christ.

1 Tim: To Timothy, a true child in the faith.

2 Tim: To Timothy, beloved child.

Titus: To Titus, a true child according to a common faith.

Phlm: To Philemon our beloved fellow-worker and Apphia the sister, and Archippus our fellow-soldier, and the church in thy house.

Three types of formulation must be distinguished. In certain cases they convey an important clue to the main thrust of the letter.

To a Church

To this category belong 1 and 2 Thessalonians, 1 and 2 Corinthians and Galatians. In these five instances the recipients are identified as "church" (*ekklēsia*).

Any contemporary of Paul would automatically have translated *ekklēsia Thessalonikeōn* in 1 and 2 Thessalonians by "the assembly of the Thessalonians" (cf. Sir 50:20) and understood it in a secular, political sense. The phrase is given a religious dimension only by the attributive *en theō patri [hēmon] kai kyriō Iēsou Christou.* The instrumental force of *en,* "in" (BDF §195, §219; Bruce 1982, 7), can only be brought out by a paraphrase: the assembly "which came into being through God the/our Father and the Lord Jesus Christ." Its origin in grace is what makes this particular assembly a "church." Here we catch a glimpse of Paul's struggle to find an appropriate Greek name for the communities he founded.

The cumbersome but necessary specification of 1 and 2 Thessalonians is neatly avoided in 1 and 2 Corinthians, which are addressed to *tē ekklēsia tou theou tē ousē en Korintō,* "to the church of God that is at Corinth." The verb "to be" here is not a mere copulative but a statement of existence (Klauck 1984, 17; Martin 1986, 3; Wolff 1989, 17). Hence, "the church of God which truly exists at Corinth." Corinth is but a visible concrete manifestation of the one Church of God (cf. 1 Cor 10:32; Acts 13:1).

The implication of this formulation, namely, that the Corinthians are neither the whole nor the only church, is immediately made explicit in the subsequent shift of attention to the members in 1 Corinthians, "those sanctified in Christ Jesus, saints in virtue of a divine call, together with all those who call on the name of our Lord Jesus Christ in every place, theirs and ours." The ambiguity of the concluding possessive pronouns has perplexed commentators, but it seems best to take them as qualifying "Lord": hence, "their Lord and ours" (NRSV, JB, NAB). Since there were others elsewhere who worshiped Jesus, and the Corinthians knew of them (cf. 1 Thess 1:7), the Corinthians should not pretend to be unique (1 Cor 4:7) and thus a law unto themselves (cf. 1 Cor 11:16; 14:36). The reader of 1 Corinthians is thereby prepared to find Paul highly critical of certain singular practices at Corinth (e.g., 1 Cor 5:1; 14:36).

The same concern to deny any uniqueness to the Corinthians surfaces in the qualification of the address of 2 Corinthians, "together with all the saints who are in the whole of Achaia." The Roman province of Achaia covered the southern third of modern Greece. Apart from Corinth the only church of which we are sure was located at Cenchreae (Rom 16:1). The improbability of the view that Paul intended the letter to be circulated throughout this huge area (Furnish 1984, 106) enhances the likelihood that the mention of believers outside Corinth was designed to remind the Corinthians that they were but part of a much wider movement.

The intimate connection between the mention of others in addition to the members of the Church at Corinth and the content of the letters renders superfluous the gratuitous hypothesis (Schnider and Stenger 1987, 23) that the "together with" clauses were added in the post-Pauline period when the letters of the apostles were collected and edited.

The influence of Paul's perception of the local situation on his formulation of the recipients is even more marked in Galatians, which is addressed *tais ekklēsiais tēs Galatias,* "to the assemblies of Galatia." He is so disappointed in the Christians there (Gal 1:6) that he is not prepared to qualify *ekklēsiai* in such a way as to give it a religious value (cf. above on 1 and 2 Thess). His negative assessment of the Galatians, perceptible from the very beginning of the letter, is underlined by the consistency with which he avoids addressing the believers as "saints."

TO THE MEMBERS OF A CHURCH

In the second type of formulation the letter is addressed, not to the Church as a whole, but to its members, who are identified as "saints." To this category belong Philippians, Romans, Colossians, and Ephesians. Why did Paul modify what had become his habitual formulation? Ephesians can be left aside, because once again it is modelled on Colossians. This is confirmed by the presence of *pistoi*, "faithful," in Ephesians, because it is in place only in Colossians where it identifies those members of the community who have not been led astray (cf. Col 2:8). Since the churches at Colossae and Rome had not been founded by Paul, it was appropriate for him to address the members as fellow believers rather than the institution as such (Abbott 1897, 194; Lohse 1968, 35).

The case of Philippians is different. Although the church was founded by Paul, the letter—more accurately one of the letters (cf. p. 8 above)—is nonetheless addressed "to the saints . . . *syn episkopois kai diakonois.*" To translate "with the bishops and deacons" (NRSV) risks giving the impression that the community was ruled by a hierarchy composed of the two orders of bishop and deacon. The presumption that this translation is the only one possible has given rise to the hypothesis that the mention of bishops and deacons is a post-Pauline interpolation (Schnider and Stenger 1987, 23). A more neutral rendering, however, is both possible and preferable, namely, "with the supervisors and ministers." Since *episkopos*, "supervisor," is attested as the designation of those entrusted with fiscal responsibilities (Gnilka 1968, 40), it is likely that the two terms refer to those who supervised the collection of financial aid for Paul and ensured the transfer to him (Phil 4:14-20; cf. 2 Cor 11:9). In this perspective it is natural that Paul should have thought, not of the community as a block, but of the individuals who had made a sacrifice to assist him.

To Individuals

The third type of formulation addresses individuals. The least ambiguous examples are found in the Pastorals where, however, there is a clear distinction between 2 Timothy and 1 Timothy/Titus. In 2 Timothy, Timothy is characterized simply as "beloved child" (cf. 1 Cor 4:17). First Timothy and Titus, however, are addressed to *gnēsiō teknō* "legitimate/authentic child," with the further qualification "in the faith" and "according to a common faith" respectively. The emphasis on their doctrinal orthodoxy contrasts with the uncomplicated affection of 2 Timothy and betrays a radically different problematic, namely, the need to counter unorthodox teaching.

With Philemon Paul associates Apphia and Archippus, and through them addresses "the church in your [sing.] house." Grammatically the possessive pronoun should refer to the proximate antecedent, which would mean that the house belonged to Archippus (so Knox 1935, ch. 3). But if this was the case, why was he not mentioned first? A patristic solution to this problem postulated that he was the son of Philemon and Apphia. This has little to recommend it save neatness. Apphia and Archippus could have been Philemon's unmarried sister and brother, or with him the leadership group of the house church.

The real problem here is the plurality of addressees, because the content shows that the letter is in fact addressed to one person (throughout the letter "you" is masculine singular). This unique phenomenon is best explained, I have suggested, as a subtle way of bringing pressure on Philemon to do what Paul required. The address ensured that the letter could not be hidden as private. Thus Paul's request became known to the other members of the church, whose sympathy with the imprisoned apostle would be expressed as criticism of Philemon if he refused to release Onesimus.

Opening Greeting

Immediately after the names of the sender(s) and recipient(s) comes the opening greeting, which must be distinguished from the greetings which form part of the conclusion. It displays a much greater uniformity that anything that has preceded it.

> *Rom:* Grace to you and peace from God our Father and the Lord Jesus Christ.
>
> *1 Cor:* Grace to you and peace from God our Father and the Lord Jesus Christ.
>
> *2 Cor:* Grace to you and peace from God our Father and the Lord Jesus Christ.

Gal:	Grace to you and peace from God our Father and the Lord Jesus Christ, who gave himself for our sins to deliver us from the present evil age, according to the will of God our Father, to whom be the glory for ever and ever. Amen.
Eph:	Grace to you and peace from God our Father and the Lord Jesus Christ.
Phil:	Grace to you and peace from God our Father and the Lord Jesus Christ.
Col:	Grace to you and peace from God our Father.
1 Thess:	Grace to you and peace.
2 Thess:	Grace to you and peace from God the Father and the Lord Jesus Christ.
1 Tim:	Grace, mercy, and peace from God the Father and Christ Jesus our Lord.
2 Tim:	Grace, mercy, and peace from God the Father and Christ Jesus our Lord.
Titus:	Grace and peace from God the Father and Christ Jesus our Savior.
Phlm:	Grace to you and peace from God the Father and the Lord Jesus Christ.

Paul never uses the secular greeting *chairein* or *salus*. In 1 Thessalonians he says "grace to you and peace." The romantic interpretation (Lohse 1968, 33) of these simple words as the Christian synthesis of the Gentile ("rejoice") and Jewish ("peace"; Milik 1953) greetings is unlikely to be correct because in 2 Thessalonians Paul feels the need to give them a specifically Christian dimension by the addition of "from God the Father and the Lord Jesus Christ." In 1 Corinthians "the Father," becomes "our Father," and in this form the greeting becomes a stereotypical feature in virtually all subsequent letters. The exceptions are Colossians and the Pastorals. For Paul the ultimate source of grace is always God. In consequence, grace cannot be a mere benign regard, as the translation "favor" might suggest, but a positive display of power better rendered by "benefaction" (Doughty 1972–73).

In Colossians the reference to the Lord Jesus Christ is lacking in the best manuscripts, even though it is found in Ephesians. No adequate explanation for the omission has been proposed. The Pastorals are not homogeneous. Titus respects the first part of the standard formula, whereas 1 and 2 Timothy modify it by the addition of "mercy" between "grace" and "peace." All three alter the second part of the stereotyped formula, 1 and 2 Timothy, by the transfer of "our" from Father to Lord, and Titus by the substitution of "our Savior" for "our Lord."

Assuming the authenticity of 2 Timothy, the addition of "mercy" is explicable as the reward to which Paul himself looked forward (cf. 1:16-18 and 4:8); it was the concrete manifestation of "the promise of the life which is in Christ Jesus" (1:1). The modified formula was then imitated by 1 Timothy which does not mention "mercy" elsewhere. The singularity of Titus is that it never speaks of Jesus Christ as "Lord," but always as "Savior" (1:4; 2:13; 3:6), an epithet which is applied an equal number of times to God (1:3; 2:10; 3:4). The intention to emphasize the intimate association of God and Jesus Christ in the work of salvation explains the reformulation of the greeting, because "God our Savior" is mentioned in the previous verse.

The ideas of "grace" and "peace" are regular features of the conclusion to Pauline letters where, however, they are split into two separate wishes (see pp. 109–10 below).

THANKSGIVING

It is a feature of Pauline letters that a thanksgiving paragraph follows the address and introduces the body of the letter. In 1 and 2 Thessalonians, 1 Corinthians, Philippians, Romans, and Colossians the first words of this paragraph are *eucharistō/omen tō theō, (mou/patri)*, "I/we give thanks to (my) God (the Father)." The formula of 2 Timothy is very close, *charin echō tō theō,* "I thank God." 2 Corinthians and Ephesians, on the contrary, have *eulogētos ho theos,* "blessed be God." No thanksgiving appears in Galatians, 1 Timothy, and Titus.

Greek Papyrus Letters

A number of Greek private letters from Egypt, ranging from the second century B.C. to the second century A.D. contain an "I give thanks to the gods" formula immediately after the standard prayer for the well-being of the person named in the address (Schubert 1939, 158–79). A perfect illustration from the lower end of this scale is furnished by a letter to his father from a young sailor in the Roman navy who had just survived a perilous crossing to Italy.

> Apion to his father and lord, Epimachos, very many greetings. Before all else I pray that you are well and that you may prosper in continual health together with my sister and her daughter and my brother. I give thanks to the Lord Seraphis [*eucharistō tōi kyriōi Sarapidi*] because when I was endangered at sea, he rescued me immediately. When I arrived at Misenum I received three gold pieces from Caesar for travelling expenses (*BGU* II, 423; White 1986, 159–60).

Some three hundred years earlier (168 B.C.) an irate wife wrote to her roaming husband, begging him to return.

> Isias to her brother Hepaestion greeting. If you are well and other things are going right, it would accord with the prayer which I make continually to the gods. (I myself and the child and all the household are in good health and think of you always.)[1] When I received your letter from Horus, in which you announce that you are in detention in the Serapeum at Memphis, for the news that you are well immediately I thanked the gods [*tois theois eucharistoun*], but I am disgusted that you have not come home, when all the others who had been secluded there have come. After having piloted myself and your child through such bad times and been driven to every extremity owing to the price of corn, I thought that now at least, with you at home, I should enjoy some respite, but you have not even thought of

---

[1] This sentence was added by Isias after the completion of the letter which she realized might be too harsh to produce the desired effect (Schubert 1939, 161).

coming home nor given any regard to our circumstances, remembering how I was in want of everything while you were still here, not to mention this long lapse of time and these critical days, during which you have sent us nothing. As, moreover, Horus who delivered the letter has brought news of your having been released, I am thoroughly ill-pleased. Notwithstanding, as your mother also is annoyed, for her sake as well as for mine please return to the city, if nothing more pressing holds you back. You will do me a favour by taking care of your bodily health. Goodbye. Year 2. Epeiph 30 (*PLond* 42; Barrett 1987, 28–29).

Schubert's analysis of the relatively small number of such letters reveals that the "I give thanks to the gods" formula was anything but a banal convention. It was used only where the parties were genuinely religious and the subject such as to arouse deep feelings (Schubert 1939, 173). It is also noticeable that what is uppermost on the writer's mind surfaces in the thanksgiving period.

These observations highlight the importance of reading the thanksgivings of the Pauline letters very carefully. They can reveal something of Paul's mental state and may convey an important clue as to the major theme(s) of the letter. They also demonstrate to what extent Paul was influenced by the formal epistolary conventions of his day. There is agreement, however, that Schubert went too far in claiming (cf. Phil 3:5) that Paul's use of the "I give thanks to God" formula proved him to be a "Hellenist of Hellenists" (1939, 184) because, if the form is Hellenistic, the content often betrays the influence of Jewish "eucharistic" formulae (Berger 1974, 219–24; O'Brien 1977, 10–11).

The Form of the Thanksgiving

Schubert is the only one to have attempted a formal description of the thanksgivings in the Pauline letters. The task was far from easy, and his conclusion betrays the inherent difficulty of accounting for all details in free-flowing compositions. He divides the Pauline thanksgivings into two basic types, the simple and the complex (1939, 35).

The *simple type* is composed of the following verbal elements in the same order: (1) I/We thank - (2) God - (3) always - (4) about you - (5) because - (6) so that. It appears in only two letters:

> (1) We are bound to give *thanks* (2) to *God* (3) *always* (4) for *you,* believers, as is fitting, (5) *because* your faith is growing abundantly and the love of everyone of you for one another is increasing, (6) *so that* we ourselves boast of you in the churches of God for your steadfastness and faith in all your persecutions and in the afflictions which you are enduring (2 Thess 1:3-4).

> (1) I give *thanks* (2) to *God* (3) *always* (4) for *you,* (5) *because* of the grace which was given you in Christ Jesus, that in every way you were enriched in him with all speech and all knowledge—even as the testimony of Christ was confirmed among you—(6) *so that* you are not lacking in any spiritual gift, as you wait for the revealing of our Lord Jesus, who will sustain you to the end, guiltless in the day of our Lord Jesus Christ. God is faithful, by whom you were called into the fellowship of his Son, Jesus Christ our Lord (1 Cor 1:4-9).

It will be immediately apparent that, while the same basic verbal grid appears in both, and is a satisfactory description of 2 Thessalonians 1:3-4, it does not adequately account for all the elements in the thanksgiving in 1 Corinthians. The utility of this exercise of formal description becomes even more problematic when we examine the second type.

The *complex type* of thanksgiving appears in 1 Thessalonians 1:2-5, Philemon 4-6, Philippians 1:3-11, Romans 1:8-15, Colossians 1:3-12, and Ephesians 1:15-19. The first four elements are identical with those in the simple type, but the remaining three elements are easier to describe than to illustrate because of the extreme verbal variations: (5) a participial construction expressing intercessory prayer, for example, "making mention of you in our prayers"; (6) a causal construction employing a verb of learning indicating the grounds for Paul's thankfulness, for example, "hearing of your faith"; (7) a clause which defies generalization save in that it concludes the thanksgiving.

When only such a generalizing description can bring out the internal coherence of a number of thanksgivings, it is obvious that any attempt to discover rigorously consistent patterns will result in self-defeating atomization. Paul was conscious of form, but more concerned with content. The literary convention of the thanksgiving, like others, was merely a frame which his versatility continuously transformed. The two essential components— Paul's gratitude and its justification—are the only totally consistent elements.

Thanksgivings in the Body of the Letter

Thanksgivings normally stand at the beginning of the body of the letter. There are, however, two exceptions in which the simple type of thanksgiving appears within the body of the letter; the numbers are those used in the description of this type above.

> And therefore (1) we give *thanks* (2) to *God* (3) *unceasingly* (5) *because* when you received the word of God which you heard from us, (4) *you* accepted it not as the word of men but as what it really is, the word of God, which is at work in you believers (1 Thess 2:13).

> But (1) we are bound to give *thanks* (2) to *God* (3) *always* (4) concerning *you,* believers beloved by the Lord, (5) *because* God chose you from the beginning to be saved through sanctification by the Spirit and belief in the truth (2 Thess 2:13).

First Thessalonians 2:13 has been explained in different ways. Schubert (1939, 26) maintains that it is part of the initial thanksgiving which, in his view, runs from 1:2 to 3:10 and in fact constitutes the body of the letter. Implausible in itself, this opinion has been refuted by J. T. Sanders (1962, 355–56).

The two thanksgivings in 1 Thessalonians suggest two beginnings. This hint was taken up by W. Schmithals (1964), who then discovered two conclusions, namely 3:11–4:2 and 5:23-28. In consequence, he argued that 1 Thessalonians was a compilation of two letters, one of which (2:13–4:2) had been inserted into the middle of the other (1:1–2:11 and 4:3–5:28). This hypothesis carries a prima facie plausibility insofar as it accounts for definite formal features, and the phenomenon of combined letters has also been seen in Philippians (cf. p. 32 above). Full confirmation, however, depends on an examination of the contents of the two letters.

Pearson, followed by Boers, has argued that 1 Thessalonians 2:13-16 is a post-Pauline interpolation. His argument from the content of verses 14-16 is strong. Paul never considered "the Jews" in general as responsible for the death of Jesus, and never viewed them as "opposed to all humanity," a common Gentile slander (Tacitus, *History,* 5.5.2). While the idea that irrevocable retribution had come upon the Jews does not necessarily refer to the fall of Jerusalem in A.D. 70, it is certainly the most natural candidate (Bruce 1982, 49). None of Pearson's serious arguments, however, apply to verses 13-14, and one could maintain equally cogently that verses 15-16 were inserted here as a development of the theme of suffering, which was also associated with the theme of imitation in the first Thanksgiving (1:6).

Schmithal's suggestion that 2 Thessalonians 2:13 is the beginning of a new letter is unconvincing. His argument is vitiated by his failure to identify a plausible letter-body and a conclusion. His example is a warning against exaggerating the implications of formal elements; in order to be a significant argument in partition theories they have to be supported by other factors.

The Absence of a Thanksgiving

The consistency of Paul's practice in 1 and 2 Thessalonians, 1 Corinthians, Philippians, Philemon, Romans, Colossians, and 2 Timothy makes the absence of thanksgivings in Galatians, 2 Corinthians, 1 Timothy and Titus significant. It represents, not irrelevant accidents, but a conscious choice.

The only explanation for the lack of any thanksgiving in Galatians is that Paul found nothing to be grateful for in the comportment of the Galatians: "I am astonished that you are so quickly deserting him who called you in the grace of Christ and turning to a different gospel" (Gal 1:6). The abruptness of the reprimand, which reinforces the secular form of the address (see above, p. 51), makes his intense agitation palpable; he is both deeply worried and profoundly disgusted. It is not unreasonable to assume that the lost "severe letter" (cf. 2 Cor 2:4) also lacked a thanksgiving. The absence of a thanksgiving in 1 Timothy (Prior 1989, 62) and Titus is not susceptible of the same explanation because there is no evidence of any animosity between sender and recipient. The lack, however, is one of the many non-Pauline features which distinguish 1 Timothy and Titus from 2 Timothy, which has a thanksgiving (Murphy-O'Connor 1991a), and is a further indication that Paul was not the author of 1 Timothy and Titus.

The introductory paragraph of 2 Corinthians begins, "Blessed be the God and Father of our Lord Jesus Christ" (1:3). The idea of thanksgiving appears only at the very end of the paragraph, "You must help us also by prayer, so that many will give thanks on our behalf" (1:11). The hint that Paul has deliberately diverged from his customary practice is borne out by a close analysis. "Ordinarily, Paul is the subject of the verb action, here it is the Corinthians; ordinarily, the addressees are referred to in the adverbial phrases, here it is Paul (*hyper hēmōn*—twice; *eis hēmas*); ordinarily the principal *eucharistō*-clause is followed by a final clause, here *eucharistō* is the verb of the final clause; ordinarily, the *eucharistō*-clause forms the beginning of the proemium, here it forms the conclusion; ordinarily, the verb is used in the active, here it is used in the passive" (Schubert 1939, 50).

The Corinthians can hardly have been unaware of the systematic way in which Paul inverted his usual pattern. Many in the community flattered themselves on their intelligence and they had one, if not two, letters with thanksgivings in their possession for comparison, namely, the "previous letter" (cf. 1 Cor 5:9) and 1 Corinthians. It would have been difficult to avoid the (correct) inference that Paul was sending them a subtle message. There is a suggestion that he cannot be unequivocally grateful for the state of the Corinthian Church. A breach has been repaired (2 Cor 7:5-16), but difficulties remain, and Paul's subversion of the normal thanksgiving prepares for similar sleight of hand with Philonic terminology in the body of 2 Corinthians 1–9 (Murphy-O'Connor 1986b).

More significantly, perhaps, Paul's unusual focus on his own experience in this introductory paragraph prefigures the major theological theme of 2 Corinthians 1–9, namely, that suffering and weakness, not power and eloquence, are the distinctive signs of the true apostle (cf. 4:7-12).

The hint of disapproval cannot explain why Ephesians also begins with a "Blessed be God" paragraph because it is immediately followed by a perfect "I give thanks" paragraph (1:15-19). All that can be suggested is that the author felt that a majestic "benediction" form with its roots deep in Judaism (Audet 1958; J. M. Robinson 1964) would be a more appropriate vehicle to introduce a letter in which continuity and novelty are perfectly blended. The eulogy, however, fulfills the function of a typical thanksgiving insofar as it lays the groundwork for basic themes of Ephesians, the cosmic perspective, the disclosure of the salvific mystery, and the role of the Spirit in living out of election (O'Brien 1979; Lincoln 1990, 18–19).

Thanksgivings as Introductions

Each of the seven regular thanksgivings is a *captatio benevolentiae* insofar as it is designed to attract the goodwill of the readers and make them more attentive and receptive. But there is no false flattery. The variety of compliments accurately reflects Paul's estimations of the qualities of the different Churches. Each thanksgiving also fulfills an introductory role in that it evokes themes which will turn out to be central to the letter.

In 1 Thessalonians 1:2-10 the basis of Paul's gratitude is the faith, hope, and charity of the Thessalonians, whereas in 2 Thessalonians 1:3-4 it is the increase of their faith and love. These virtues are all the more manifest and their growth all the more significant because of the persecution which they are enduring. This emphasis suggests that a major concern of the letters will be to reinforce that steadfastness in various ways, but no hints of specific developments are given.

When compared with 1 and 2 Thessalonians, 1 Corinthians 1:4-9 is remarkable for what it does not say. The most Paul can find on which to compliment the Corinthians is their possession of the spiritual gifts of "speech" and "knowledge," of which he has no high opinion (1 Cor 8:1; 13:8-9; 14:2-5), and the fact that they were "called" into fellowship. The absence of any reference to "love" and its expression in true "fellowship" hints that this call has not really been answered. Much of the letter is in fact concerned with large and small divisions within the community (1:10–4:21; 6:1-11; 11:17-34), and disputes on doctrinal (15:1-59) and ethical matters (6:12–7:40) "Knowledge," particularly as applied to meat offered to idols, is dealt with in chapters 8–10, whereas inspired "speech" is the subject of chapters 12–14. The epistolary function of the thanksgiving is perfectly realized.

In Philemon 4-6 Paul's gratitude is stimulated by Philemon's faith in Christ and his love which is directed towards "all the saints" (BDF §477[2]). In terms of epistolary function the key word in the controverted next verse is *koinōnia* (O'Brien 1977, 54-58). We catch a hint that Philemon will be expected to share something. In fact he will be invited to release his slave Onesimus.

Koinōnia is also the key word in Philippians 1:3-11 but there it connotes the apostolic partnership through which grace works, and which is the reason for Paul's thanksgiving. Is Philippians 1:3-11 an introduction to the rest of the letter? The answer is complicated by the fact that the integrity of Philippians is not guaranteed. It has been argued that the thanksgiving introduces the themes of joy, love, knowledge, and suffering as witness, which are found in all the postulated letters. Contrary to some claims (Jewett 1970), this does not prove the unity of the epistle. The concerns are fundamental and one would expect them to surface in letters to the same community, particularly if written in proximity to one another. In another analysis the themes of the thanksgiving are concentrated in the letter made up of 1:3-3:1 and 4:2-9 (O'Brien 1977, 37-40).

Romans was written to a community with which Paul was not personally acquainted. All he knew was that there were Christians there, and that is what he is thankful for: "your faith is proclaimed in all the world" (1:8). Once again, the thanksgiving evokes the major theological and personal themes of the letter, namely, the mediating sonship of Christ as the basic element of the gospel, ministerial obligation flowing from salvific debt, and on the personal level Paul's planned visit to Rome (O'Brien 1977, 224-29).

As in his first letter, the thanksgiving in Colossians 1:3-14 ascribes Paul's gratitude to the faith, hope, and charity of those among the Colossians who have remained faithful. The letter, it will be recalled, is addressed not to "the saints" (as in Rom and Phil) but to "the faithful among the saints" (1:2). This is the sole occasion on which Paul makes such a distinction in order to find a genuine compliment. His progress in diplomacy, by comparison with Galatians, is evident in the fact that he does not explicitly mention the problem of false teachers until 2:6. Such restraint means that the real problem with which the letter deals surfaces in the thanksgiving only in the discrete introduction of "truth" to qualify both the gospel and its perception and of "spiritual" to define wisdom and understanding. The emphasis on the universality and fruitfulness of the gospel implicitly condemns the sterile parochialism of the Colossian heresy.

The last thanksgiving to be discussed is that of 2 Timothy 1:3-5. Most exceptionally the basic ground for Paul's gratitude is not a religious virtue but the friendship which binds him to Timothy, whose sincere faith is mentioned only in second place. The theme of the letter is announced both explicitly by the admonition to "kindle the gift of God which is within you"—Timothy must take a new grip on his leadership role (Prior 1989, 64)—and implicitly by Paul's longing to see Timothy (cf. 4:9), which would get him away from Ephesus where his ministry had been less than successful.

THE BODY OF THE LETTER

Only one effort has been made to offer a formal description of the body of the Pauline letter. According to J. L. White, the letter-body is composed of "a formal opening, connective and transitional formulae, concluding 'eschatological climax' and apostolic *parousia* . . . paraenesis" (1972, 71). His pioneering effort, however, focused exclusively on the detection of repeated literary formulas. This led to neglect of the content, and nothing concrete regarding the letter as a whole in fact emerges from his analysis.

Others used the same formal approach but made no pretence of accounting for the complete body of the letter. Their interest was in the detection of formulaic features similar to those found in the address and conclusion of the letters (Mullins 1972; Schnider and Stenger 1987). Thus there are studies of

—introductory formulae (White 1971);
—disclosure formulae (Mullins 1964);
—request formulae (Bjerkelund 1967);
—confidence formulae (Olsen 1984, 1985);
—benedictions (Jewett 1969; Mullins 1977);
—rhetorical questions (Wuellner 1986; Watson 1989);
—transition techniques (Roberts 1986);
—autobiographical statements (Lyons 1985);
—travel plans (Funk 1967; Mullins 1973);
—comparison, self-praise, and irony (Forbes 1986).

The list could be extended and yet be incomplete. The benefit of these studies has been in their clarification of details and the furnishing of parallels, which once again demonstrate to what extent Paul was part of the first-century epistolary world.

Rhetorical Criticism of Letters

In recent years a different approach to the letter as a whole has made its mark in Pauline studies. Efforts, stimulated by the research of G. A. Kennedy (1984), have been made to characterize Paul's letters and to analyze their contents in terms of the conventions of ancient rhetoric and epistolography. The two are not identical but, since the letter was but a substitute for speech, techniques and forms of verbal communication had an influence on written communication (Aune 1987, 160–61). Moreover, it should be remembered, Paul's letters were designed to be read aloud (1 Thess 5:27; Col 4:16).

The Three Types of Oratory

Oratory is the art of persuasion. At all times and in all places the ability to win others to one's point of view has been esteemed. In no sphere does its importance need to be emphasized, be it business, politics, law, or courtship. In the democratic societies of Greece and Rome, success in public life depended on seductive eloquence. Dictators might come and go, but invitation remained the hallmark of civilization, and the characteristic of the educated person. While some practitioners were naturally gifted in finding the key to an audience's heart, the majority were not, and the ambitious sought to codify persuasion into a science that the diligent could master. The search began in the fifth century B.C. (Kennedy 1963, 58–61), and the importance of the matter was such that the different types of oratory continued to be vigorously debated in the first century. After summarizing the discussion, Quintilian (A.D. 35–ca. 95) concludes:

> The safest and most rational course seems to be to follow the authority of the majority. There is, then, as I have said, one kind concerned with praise and blame, which, however, derives its name from the better of its two functions and is called *laudatory;* others however call it *demonstrative.* Both names are believed to be derived from the Greek in which the corresponding terms are *ecomiastic* and *epideictic.* . . . But it may be that the Romans are not borrowing from Greek when they apply the title *demonstrative,* but are merely led to do so because praise and blame demonstrate the nature of the object with which they are concerned. The second kind is *deliberative,* the third *forensic* oratory (*Institutio Oratoria* 3:4.12-15; Butler).

He does not clarify the last two because he is reserving their definitions for a later point in his work.

> The *deliberative* department of oratory (also called the *advisory* department), while it deliberates about the future, also enquires about the past, while its functions are twofold and consist in advising and persuading (*Institutio Oratoria* 3:8.6; Butler).

> Now concerning the *forensic* kind of oratory, which presents the utmost variety, but whose duties are no more than two, the bringing and rebutting of charges (*Institutio Oratoria* 3:9.1; Butler).

This tripartite division was shared by Greeks and Romans because the tradition it represents goes back to Aristotle (384–322 B.C.), whose text clarifies what Quintilian says.

The types of rhetoric are three because that is the number of the types of audience. For a speech is composed of three factors—the speaker, the subject and the listener—and it is to the last of these that its purpose is related.

Now the listener must be either a spectator or a judge, and, if a judge, one either of the past or of the future. The judge about the future is the assembly member. The judge about the past is the juror. And the assessor of the orator's capacity is the spectator.

So that there must needs be three types of rhetorical speech, deliberative, forensic, and display [or: demonstrative].

The kinds of *deliberation* are exhortation and deterrence. For, in all cases, both those who privately advise and those who address the people at large are doing one or the other of these.

The kinds of *forensic oratory* are prosecution and defence, in one or the other of which the litigants must perforce be engaged.

The kinds, finally, of *display speaking* are praise and denigration.

The time-orientations of each are different. For the deliberator it is the future, because it is about what is to be that he deliberates, whether urging or dissuading. For the litigant it is the past, because both prosecution and defence make claims about what has happened. For the display orator the present is the most important because it is on the basis of how things are that all accord praise or blame, though they also often make additional use of historical recollection or anticipatory conjecture.

Each of the types of oratory has a different objective. . . . The objective of the deliberative orator is advantage or harm. To exhort is to urge as being more advantageous. To deter is to dissuade as being more harmful. Other aspects such as justice or nobility are ancillary.

The objective of the forensic speaker is justice and injustice, though he too will bring in other aspects as ancillaries.

The objective of the display orator is nobility and baseness, to which speakers also relate the other aspects (*Rhetoric* 1:2.3; 1358b; Lawson-Tancred adapted).

The density of this description, in which not a word is wasted, may impede comprehension. Hence a graphic summary may be helpful.

DELIBERATIVE ORATORY

Objective	To secure the adoption or repudiation of a course of action
Method	Persuasion or dissuasion
Hearers	Have to make a decision
Time	Future

FORENSIC ORATORY

Objective	To ensure that justice is done
Method	Attack or defense
Hearers	Have to make a decision
Time	Past

DISPLAY ORATORY

Objective	To celebrate common values by proving someone worthy of honor or the reverse
Method	Praise or blame
Hearers	Simple observers of orator's skill
Time	Present

The exclusiveness of these descriptions betrays their artificiality. They are derived *a priori* from a consideration of possibilities and not *a posteriori* from the analysis of actual speeches. Reality is never quite as neat as the distinctions the mind makes. A purely didactic speech (e.g., a class), or a consolatory discourse (e.g., on the occasion of a major disaster) do not fit easily or naturally into the above schema. The point is made with force by Quintilian:

> On what kind of oratory are we to consider ourselves to be employed, when we complain, console, pacify, excite, terrify, encourage, instruct, explain obscurities, narrate, plead for mercy, thank, congratulate, reproach, abuse, describe, command, retract, express our desires and opinions, to mention no other of the many possibilities? (*Institutio Oratoria* 3:4.3; Butler).

The different types could also be mixed, as when an orator flatters a judge as part of his effort to secure an acquittal, or when a future good is praised. Inevitably there are debates (often futile) as to the correct terminology to employ, and confusion is engendered by the illegitimate extension of meaning. Thus to overemphasize the educational dimension in display discourse makes it indistinguishable from deliberative rhetoric.

THE RHETORICAL CLASSIFICATION OF THE PAULINE LETTERS

In opposition to Cicero, who wrote regularly to his friend Atticus just for the sheer pleasure of communication, Paul never put pen to paper except when it was absolutely imperative. A letter for him always had a definite goal; he designed it to accomplish something. Lacking any mechanism to impose his will, he could not enforce; he was inescapably bound to persuasion. Hence scholars have had to raise and attempt to answer the question: to which of the three categories of oratory do the Pauline letters belong?

H. D. Betz (1979, 14–25) argued that Galatians is an apologetic letter which systematically uses the conventions of forensic oratory. The hypothesis has not gone unchallenged, and the basic criticism is that Betz has attempted to interpret the whole in terms of one of its parts. Paul is defending himself in Galatians 1–2, and his technique is forensic, but not in the remainder of the letter, whose thrust is deliberative (Kennedy 1984, 144–45; Hall 1987; Smit 1989; Longenecker 1990, cxiii).

The major objection to Betz's position is the long *exhortatio,* "exhortation" (5:1–6:10)—this and other technical terms for parts of a speech are explained in the next section—which has no place in forensic oratory. Moreover, he cannot produce any example of a forensic letter, whereas Galatians has an almost perfect parallel in the deliberative discourse of Demosthenes *On Peace* (Vouga 1988). The extended *narratio,* "narration" (1:12–2:14), however, is not normal in a deliberative discourse. Clearly Galatians does not fit neatly into either of the classical categories, and this has to be kept in mind while recognizing that its basic thrust is deliberative insofar as the concern of the letter is corrective persuasion.

The concern of Colossians is parallel to that of Galatians, insofar as both are designed to reform communities tainted by false teaching by persuading them of the error of their ways. Consequently, it too should be seen as an example of deliberative oratory.

Wuellner (1987, 460) considers 1 Corinthians to be demonstrative, because it is educational, but since virtually all its content is concerned with changes in belief and practice it is more correctly treated by Kennedy, who classifies 1 Corinthians and 2 Corinthians 8–9 as deliberative, while maintaining that 2 Corinthians 1–7 and 10–13 are forensic (1984, 87, 93). The latter is above all an explosive venting of Paul's bitter disappointment which exhibits little concern for the feelings of the recipients; it is better classed as a speech for the defense than anything else. When properly understood, however, 2 Corinthians 1–7 is less a defense of Paul's apostolate than a sustained and subtle effort to dissuade the spirit-people from their alliance with the Judaizers and at the same time to persuade them to adopt the apostle's perspective. In 2:14–4:6 the appeal to their self-interest is unmistakable (Murphy-O'Connor 1986b). I would prefer, therefore, to class 2 Corinthians 1–7 as deliberative.

Kennedy (1984, 142–44) considers 1 and 2 Thessalonians to be deliberative. Jewett (1986a, 82) concurs as regards 2 Thessalonians, but points out that in 1 Thessalonians Paul explicitly expresses his satisfaction with the Thessalonians (4:1); such praise is designed to reinforce their present status. Thus 1 Thessalonians, he maintains, should be considered an example of display rhetoric (1986, 71–72). However justified this classification may be in theoretical terms, it is manifest that a huge abyss separates 1 Thessalonians from the classic display discourses of, for example, Dio Chrysostom or Aelius Aristides (a sample is given in Murphy-O'Connor 1992, 119–22). Care in the use of terminology is as imperative as a hermeneutic of suspicion in its comprehension.

Kennedy (1984, 152) identifies Romans as demonstrative. This might be tenable if Romans were a theological position paper unrelated to the specific situation in Rome, because Paul certainly intends to affirm common values and to display his gospel. But once it is conceded, as Kennedy appears to do, that the purpose of the letter is to introduce Paul's gospel to the Roman Church in such a way as to make himself welcome and at the same time to dissipate misunderstandings and to defuse potential opposition, it seems clear that Romans, if anything (Aune 1987, 219), is deliberative. Paul has a thesis to argue (Rom 1:16-17). Thus the letter is necessarily persuasive and forward looking (Aletti 1991, 31–53). Philippians, according to Kennedy (1984, 77), is largely demonstrative. This assessment, however, applies only to one of the component letters, namely, 1:3–3:1 and 4:2-9. Paul's concern for future developments is the dominant feature of 3:2–4:1 which, in consequence, should be treated as deliberative. So also Philemon which is designed to persuade Philemon to release Onesimus (Church 1978).

No satisfactory attempt has been made to categorize Ephesians, whose general character gives it a unique position. The first three chapters celebrate the present gifts of the readers as recipients of the benefits of the divine plan of salvation. To this extent, it is demonstrative. The three final chapters, however, are a developed appeal to live in conformity with these realities, and as such belong to the deliberative genre.

Since the Pastorals are formally addressed to individuals, they cannot be considered as speeches and so escape rhetorical classification.

The diversity displayed by this brief survey reveals one of the major dangers of rhetorical criticism. The classification of a letter is usually based on an impression of the contents, justified perhaps by one or two features, not on a detailed analysis of the whole argument. This, as Aletti (1992, 390) emphasizes, is to put the cart before the horse. Moreover, it becomes apparent that the complexity of any given letter is ill-served by the unsophisticated application of univocal categories.

THE COMPONENTS OF A DELIBERATIVE SPEECH

If, on occasion, Paul had to discriminate between truth and falsehood, his permanent concern was to persuade his readers of the value of particular courses of action, all of which, in his mind, were but manifestations of the constraining love of Christ (2 Cor 5:14). It is imperative, therefore, to examine in some detail the constitutive elements of deliberative and forensic discourse.

In 55 B.C. Cicero published *De Oratore,* in which he distilled the experience of a life of successful oratory. In it he dismisses

as immature a similar work, *De Inventione,* written some thirty
years earlier; it was, he says, merely a hasty and incomplete working up of the notes he had taken when studying rhetoric (*De Oratore* 1:2.5). The criticism is repeated by Quintilian, *Institutio
Oratoria* 3:6.59. The same course of lectures, it is thought,
provided another set of class-notes which an unknown author developed into a work known as the *Rhetorica ad Herennium,* addressed to Gaius Herennius sometime between 86 and 82 B.C.
(Kennedy 1972, 103–48). The author is unknown, but the name
L. Hirtuleius has been persuasively argued (Achard 1989, xxxii
n. 161).

This latter study is the first complete Latin manual and
represents a conscious effort to adapt the Greek rhetorical tradition, and particularly that of Rhodes, to Roman needs. "Our author gives us a Greek art in Latin dress, combining a Roman spirit
with Greek doctrine" (Caplan, vii). It thus provides invaluable
insights into the sort of rhetorical influence to which Paul was
subjected. The next really significant contribution, after the works
of Cicero's maturity—*Oratoriae Partitiones* (ca. 54 B.C.), *De Op-
timo Genere Oratorum* (52 B.C.), *De Claris Oratoribus* (46 B.C.),
and *Topica* (44 B.C.)—was the *Institutio Oratoria* of Marcus
Famius Quintilianus, which appeared in the last decade of the first
century A.D.

The standardization of rhetorical practice around the turn of
the era is evident in the uniformity of these representative manuals
regarding the art of oratory. All agree that a fully qualified speaker
needed to be a master of five skills. Let Quintilian be the spokes-
man: "The art of oratory, as taught by most authorities, and those
the best, consists of five parts: invention, arrangement, style,
memory and delivery" (*Institutio Oratoria* 3:3.1; Butler). The last
three need no explanation. The words had to be well chosen, the
composition grammatically correct, and the tone appropriate to
the occasion. Then it had to be remembered accurately, and spoken clearly with appropriate gestures. "Invention" in those days
did not imply creativity, as it does today, but rather ingenuity
in "finding out" effective arguments and suitable illustrations.
"Arrangement" (in Latin, *dispositio*; in Greek, *taxis*) referred to
the basic schema which was considered to be the framework of
all deliberative and forensic discourse. Precisely the same elements

have been detected in letters ranging from Plato to Seneca (Probst 1991, 55–107). Modern scholars have detected this outline in the Pauline letters. Hence it is necessary to explain the schema in some detail before examining the use that has been made of it. As regards the "arrangement" of a discourse, Aristotle, with his flair for highlighting the essential, said:

> There are two parts in any speech. It is necessary both to state the subject matter and to demonstrate it. . . . The necessary sections of a speech, then, are *presentation* and *proof*. They are the elements which properly belong to a discourse, but the maximum number of parts are *introduction, presentation, proof* and *epilogue* (*Rhetoric* 3:13; 1414ab; Lawson-Tancred adapted).

A certain impatience is palpable. Aristotle was in fact reacting against the facile multiplication of subdivisions. His sobriety unfortunately had little effect on his successors.

Modern authors tend to use Latin terminology for the parts of a speech and I shall do likewise, not only because such language appears in commentaries and articles, but also because of the risk of confusion caused by the profusion of possible English equivalents. In the above text from Aristotle the Latin equivalents of his four parts are respectively, *exordium, narratio, probatio* (or *confirmatio,* or *argumentatio*), and *peroratio*. Other elements have been added from the classical rhetorical manuals because they are helpful when dealing with Paul's letters.

Exordium

The introduction to the speech is named, not surprisingly, the *exordium*. Its function is to focus the attention of the audience and to obtain its goodwill. This can be done in four ways, by restrained self-promotion on the part of the speaker indicating the justice of his claim to speak, by criticizing opponents, by praise of the audience, which should not be fulsome, and by the attractive way the issue is outlined.

Narratio

The next section is usually the *narratio,* which is designed to display the facts which constitute the background of the issue.

It must be brief, clear, and probable. Nothing essential may be omitted. Anything to the speaker's disadvantage should be glossed over lightly, whereas favorable points should be brought out as forcefully as possible.

The extent to which the *exordium* and *narratio* should be developed depends on the relationship of the speaker to the audience and the level of their understanding of the issues. The speaker who is already held in respect does not have to win it. If he and the audience agree on the facts, he does not have to recite them. To waste time on the evident has an alienating effect. As regards a deliberative speech Aristotle appositely noted:

> Narration is least common in deliberative oratory, as none relates what is to come; but if there should be narration, let it be of past facts, so that in recalling them men may judge better for the future (*Rhetoric* 3:16; 1417b; Lawson-Tancred).

Digressio

This part is not integral to the discourse, and is designed to win the favor of the hearers by giving them a break from the concentration required to follow the *narratio* and which will be necessary again in the *probatio/confirmatio/argumentatio*. It is a moment when the speaker can give free rein to his talent in order to delight the audience, but the subject matter should be related somehow to the theme of the discourse.

Propositio

The next step is for the speaker to define the precise thesis for which he is going to argue. This is called the *propositio*. If the thesis is complicated, the speaker should define its component elements in a *partitio,* which is a division of the thesis into separate headings.

Confirmatio

The main body of the discourse is the *confirmatio*—often called the *probatio* or *argumentatio*—in which the *propositio* is established. In the deliberative mode there is no question of proving the truth, as there is in the forensic mode. Of its very nature deliberative oratory deals with questions on which certitude prior to action is impossible. Only when a chosen course of action has been pursued and all its consequences have become apparent can a definitive decision on its value be made. That point, however, lies far in the future. Here and now, in the present, the speaker is concerned only with the better, showing that in given circumstances one course of action is preferable to another. How should one go about it? The answer given by Aristotle has never been improved upon, being based on the three universal factors found in all forms of discourse—the speaker, the listener, and the word.

> Of those proofs that are furnished through the speech there are three kinds. Some reside in the character of the speaker [*ethos*], some in a certain disposition of the audience [*pathos*] and some in the speech itself [*logos*], through its demonstrating or seeming to demonstrate.
>
> Proofs from character are produced whenever the speech is given in such a way as to render the speaker worthy of credence. We more readily and sooner believe reasonable people on all matters in general and absolutely on questions where precision is impossible and two views can be maintained. But this effect too must come about in the course of the speech, not through the speaker's being believed in advance to be of a certain character. Unlike some experts, we do not exclude the speaker's reasonable image from the art as contributing nothing to persuasiveness. On the contrary, character contains almost the strongest proof of all, so to speak.
>
> Proofs from the disposition of the audience are produced whenever they are induced by the speech into an emotional state. We do not give judgement in the same way when aggrieved and when pleased, in sympathy and in revulsion. . . .
>
> Finally, proof is achieved by the speech, when we demonstrate either a real or an apparent persuasive aspect of each particular matter (*Rhetoric* 1:2; 1356a; Lawson-Tancred).

The second and third points need brief commentary. The form of speech which touches the emotions is the *exhortatio,* which can be inserted where it seems most appropriate.

The deliberative discourse is essentially comparative, and success depends on convincing the audience that the *propositio* is supported both by honor and advantage. In one way or another the proposed course of action is held to reflect the cardinal virtues of prudence, justice, fortitude, and temperance and that it is in the self-interest of the audience. The difficulty of the *confirmatio* is the possible tension between the honorable and the useful. What is expedient may not be the honorable course, and what is honorable may not offer any advantage.

Intimately bound up with the *confirmatio* is its antithesis, the *refutatio,* in which the alternative course of action is presented in the most unattractive light possible. It is shown to be not only base and useless, but dangerous, unpleasant, and unprofitable. Ideally the *refutatio* follows the *confirmatio,* but in practice they are often intertwined.

How exactly are the various points established logically? Once again Aristotle provides the answer.

> All exponents produce demonstrative proofs by the production either of examples or of enthymemes, and of nothing else besides. . . . The demonstration that something is so from many similar cases is in logic called induction, but in rhetoric example. The demonstration from the fact that, if certain conditions obtain, then something else beyond them will result because of them, and through their obtaining, either in general or for the most part, is called deduction in logic and enthymeme in rhetoric (*Rhetoric* 1:2; 1356b; Lawson-Tancred adapted).

In other words, proof must be either inductive or deductive and, since the matter is contingent, the framework is probability. Certitude is not to be looked for. The force of examples derives from the assumption that if something has been so in the past, it is so in the present and will be so in the future, human nature being a constant. The only difference between a syllogism and an enthymeme is explicitness. In dialectic every element of the argument must be spelled out explicitly. In rhetoric, on the contrary, it is not only permissible but preferable to rely on unstated common ground between the speaker and hearers. This in fact is what is implied in the word *enthymeme*. It is the transcription of the

Greek *enthymēma* which is a combination of *en* "in," and
thymos, "mind." To assume that something is held "in the mind"
of the audience is a compliment which has its own persuasive
force.

Peroratio

The deliberative speech concludes with a *peroratio*. In it the
speaker recapitulates his arguments (*enumeratio*), incites the audience to hatred of the refused alternative (*indignatio*), and strives
to win the pity of his hearers (*conquestio*).

THE RHETORICAL SCHEMA APPLIED TO THE PAULINE LETTERS

The clarity of the above outline is due to the fact that it is a
description of what is theoretically best. As noted before, however, reality does not always conform to the ideal. Neither do real
discourses always reflect the lineaments of the perfect model.
Moreover, what Paul wrote were letters, not speeches. The creation of showcases for his rhetorical skills was not his prime consideration. Nonetheless a number of exegetes have attempted to
display the way the parts of a deliberative discourse are realized
in certain letters (Wuellner 1979, 177–88). I have conformed their
terminology to that explained above.

Romans
W. Wuellner (1976)
Exordium: 1:1-15; Transitus: 1:16-17; Confirmatio: 1:18–15:13;
Peroratio: 15:14–16:23.
G. A. Kennedy (1984, 153–54)
Exordium: 1:8-15; Propositio: 1:16-17; Confirmatio: 1:18–
11:36; Exhortatio: 12:1–15:13; Peroratio: 15:14-23.
R. Jewett (1986b)
Exordium: 1:1-12; Narratio: 1:13-15; Propositio: 1:16-17; Con-
firmatio: 1:18–15:13; Peroratio: 15:14–16:23.

1 Corinthians
M. Mitchell (1991, 184–86)
Epistolary Prescript: 1:1-3; Exordium: 1:4-9; Propositio: 1:10;
Narratio: 1:11-17; Confirmatio: 1:18–15:57; Peroratio: 15:58;
Epistolary Conclusion: 16:1-24.

Galatians

H. D. Betz (1979, 16–23)
Exordium: 1:6-11; Narratio: 1:12–2:14; Propositio: 2:15-21;
Confirmatio: 3:1–4:31 (Digressio: 3:19-25); Exhortatio: 5:1–
6:10; Epistolary postscript: 6:11-18.

R. G. Hall
Exordium: 1:1-5; Propositio: 1:6-9; Confirmatio: 1:10–6:10;
Peroratio: 6:11-18.

J. Smit[2]
Exordium: 1:6-12; Narratio: 1:13–2:21; Confirmatio: 3:1–4:11;
Peroratio: 4:12–5:12; Amplificatio: 6:11-18.

G. A. Kennedy (1984, 148–51)
Exordium: 1:6-10; Confirmatio: 1:11–5:1; Exhortatio: 5:2-6:10;
Peroratio: 6:11-18.

F. Vouga
Exordium: 1:6-11; Narratio: 1:12–2:14; Propositio: 2:14-21;
Confirmatio: 3:1–4:31; Exhortatio: 5:1–6:10.

B. L. Mack (1990, 69–72)
Exordium: 1:6-10; Narratio: 1:11–2:14; Propositio: 2:14–3:5;
Confirmatio: 3:6–4:7; Exhortatio: 4:8-20.

M. Bachmann (1992, 158)
Exordium: 1:6-10; Narratio: 1:11–2:14 (14b is a partitio); Confirmatio: 2:15–6:17; Eschatokoll: 6:18.

Philippians
D. F. Watson (1988)
Exordium: 1:3-26; Narratio; 1:27-30; Confirmatio: 2:1–3:21;
Peroratio: 4:1-20.

Colossians
J.-N. Aletti (1993, 39)
Exordium: 1:3-23 (1:21-23 is a partitio); Confirmatio: 1:24–
4:1; Peroratio: 4:2-6.

1 Thessalonians
R. Jewett (1986a, 72–76)
Exordium: 1:1-5; Narratio: 1:6–3:13; Confirmatio: 4:1–5:22;
Peroratio: 5:23-28

[2] Smit considers that Gal 5:13–6:10, though written by Paul, was not part of the original letter.

F. W. Hughes (Jewett 1986a, 221)

Exordium: 1:1-10; Narratio: 2:1-3:10; Partitio: 3:11-13; Confirmatio: 4:1-5:5; Peroratio: 5:4-11; Exhortatio: 5:12-22; Conclusio: 5:23-28.

G. A. Kennedy (1984, 142-44)

Exordium: 1:2-10; Refutatio: 2:1-8; Narratio: 2:9-3:13; Confirmatio: 4:1-5:22; Peroratio: 5:23-28.

2 Thessalonians

R. Jewett (1986a, 82-85)

Exordium: 1:1-12; Partitio: 2:1-2; Confirmatio: 2:3-3:5; Exhortatio: 3:6-15; Peroratio: 3:16-18.

F. W. Hughes

Exordium: 1:1-12; Partitio: 2:1-2; Confirmatio: 2:3-15; Peroratio: 2:16-17; Exhortatio: 3:1-15; Epistolary postscript: 3:16-18.

G. Holland (Jewett 1986a, 225)

Exordium: 1:3-4; Narratio: 1:5-12; Confirmatio: 2:1-17; Exhortatio: 3:1-13; Peroratio: 3:14-15; Epistolary postscript: 3:16-18.

Philemon

F. F. Church

Exordium: 4-7; Confirmatio: 8-16; Peroratio: 17-22.

Before discussing the validity of such analyses attention must be drawn to one unfortunate consequence of the application of the rhetorical schema.

MISUSE OF THE RHETORICAL SCHEMA

Refusal to acknowledge the truth of what Quintilian said (see p. 86 below) has led to the use of the rhetorical schema for an end for which it was never intended, namely, to demonstrate the limits of a literary unity with a view to establishing its original independence.

G. A. Kennedy divides 2 Corinthians 1-7 as follows: Exordium: 1:3-8; Narratio: 1:8-2:13; Propositio and Partitio: 2:14-17; Confirmatio: 3:1-6:13; Peroratio: 7:2-16. Mistakenly treating 6:14-7:1 as an interpolation (see Murphy-O'Connor 1988), he concludes: "The letter is rhetorically complete at this point. All of its topics and headings have been fully explored, and the end has been linked to the beginning'' (1984, 91). He then goes on to ask: "Can chapters 8 and 9 possibly be part of the same letter as chapters 1–7? The juxtaposition of the two blocks of text is rhetorically unsatisfactory: 1–7 is too long to serve as an introduction to 8–9, and yet 8–9 is too developed to be a kind of postscript to 1–7." Thus he concludes that we have to do with two separate letters, both brought by Titus, who was instructed to withhold 8–9 until he was sure that 1–7 had been well received (1984, 92).

The unstated assumption essential to this argument is that Paul felt himself bound by the laws of rhetoric to the point where he could not have written 2 Corinthians 8–9 after 2 Corinthians 1–7. The great stylist and theorist Cicero was not so circumscribed, as some simple statistics demonstrate. His postscript in *QFr* 3 is 41 percent of the length of the original letter, that in *Att* 12:28–29.1 is 32 percent of the length of the original letter, whereas (calculated in verses) 2 Corinthians 8–9 is only 28 percent of the length of 2 Corinthians 1–7. Why could Paul not have done as Cicero did? Is it not probable that Paul possessed the "wise adaptability" of Quintilian, and was fully capable of ignoring rhetorical conventions when it suited him? Issues were what mattered, not appearances.

H. D. Betz (1985) has used rhetorical theory in an attempt to prove that 2 Corinthians 8–9 were originally independent letters. The logic of his argument is simple. If chapters 8 and 9 can be thought of as separate letters, then they were so in fact. But, he claims, both exhibit the same structure: Exordium: 8:1–5 and 9:1–2; Narratio: 8:6 and 9:3–5a; Propositio: 8:7–8 and 9:5b–c; Probatio: 8:9–15 and 9:6–14; Commendation of Delegates: 8:16–23; Peroratio: 8:24 and 9:15. Hence, originally they must have been independent documents.

The fundamental objection to this argument touches the accuracy of Betz's analysis. S. K. Stowers, an expert in epistolary rhetoric, perceptively commented: "It stretches the imagination beyond belief to think of 8:6 or 9:3–5a as a *narratio*. What is the point of calling the prayer of thanksgiving in 9:15 a *peroratio*? The only good answer is that Betz is determined to describe chapter 8 as an autonomous discourse" (1987, 730).[3] Betz's classifi-

---

[3] The same objection applies to Mack's (1990, 59–60) division of 2 Cor

cation, in other words, furnishes a perfect illustration of the distortion which occurs when Pauline material is forced to fit into an alien rhetorical mold. Betz's observations lead only to the simple conclusion that when Paul had to deal with an administrative problem he went about it in a business-like way. I shall return to this point below. Much more attention along these lines has been accorded to 1 Corinthians. H. Probst has made a valiant effort to fit all the major sections of the letter to the rhetorical schema. Others, however, have attempted it for parts of the letter, notably B. Standaert (1983), R. Pesch (1986),[4] B. L. Mack (55–66), and H. Merklein (109–13). Their conclusions can be tabulated as follows:

1 Cor 1–4	Exord	Narrat	Prob I	Peror I	Prob II	Peror II
Pesch	1:10-17	1:18–2:16	3:1-17	3:18-23	4:1-13	4:14-21
Probst	1:10-31	2:1–3:4	3:5-17			3:18–4:21
Merklein	1:10-17	1:18–2:16	3:1-17	3:18-21	4:1-13	4:14-21

1 Cor 5–6						
Probst	5:1-5	5:6-11	5:12–6:11			6:12-20

1 Cor 8–10						
Probst	8:1-13	9:1-18	9:19–10:17			10:18–11:1

1 Cor 9						
Pesch	9:1-3	9:4-14	9:15-23			9:24-27

1 Cor 12–14						
Standaert	12:1-11	12:12-31 + 13:1-13	14:1-36			14:37-40
Probst	12:1-11	12:12-31	13:1–14:25			14:26-40

1 Cor 15						
Pesch	15:1-3a	15:3b-11	15:12-28	15:29-34	15:35-49	15:50-58
Probst	15:1-3a	15:3b-11	15:12-34			15:35-58
Mack	15:1-2	15:3-20	15:21-50			15:51-58

None of these scholars invokes the rhetorical schema for the same purpose. Probst bases his conclusion that 1 Corinthians 1–4, 5–6, 8–10, 12–14, and 15 were originally independent letters on

9 into: Exordium: 9:1-2, Narratio: 9:3-5; Confirmatio: 9:6-10; Exhortatio: 9:11-14: Conclusio: 9:15.
[4] The conclusions of Pesch coincide in detail with those of Bünker, as reported by Probst (1991, 306, 334).

the sole fact that each embodies the schema. On the basis of contradictions and repetitions, Pesch divides 1 Corinthians into four letters: (A) 1:1-5:8 + 6:1-11; (B) 5:9-13 + 6:12-20 + 10:1-11:34; (C) 15:1-58; and (D) 7:1-9:27 + 12:1-14:40 + 16:1-24. Then to support his hypothesis, but not to found it as in the case of Probst, he claims that one of the letters so reconstructed exhibits the rhetorical schema. Standaert and Mack make no claims regarding the integrity of 1 Corinthians and are concerned exclusively with the articulation of Paul's thought in various parts of the letter.

The basis of Pesch's dissection of 1 Corinthians does not resist close examination. The contradictions and repetitions he discerns are either forced or non-existent, and his justification of the editorial process whereby the letters were taken apart and reassembled is implausible. The one positive contribution of his work is to show that classical source criticism provides no justification for denying the literary integrity of 1 Corinthians.

It is not possible to discuss all of Probst's hypotheses; one example must suffice. The text which he analyzes in the most detail, 1 Corinthians 8-10, illustrates the danger of his approach because the rhetorical categories do not always accurately describe what Paul is doing. Probst defines 8:1-13 as the *exordium*. But these verses are not an introduction to what follows. They are a complete treatment of the issue of meat offered to idols, in which Paul dissects the arguments of his opponents (an aspect which Probst ignores) and provides a fully reasoned basis for the choice of an appropriate course of action. While 9:1-6 might have some claim to be considered a *narratio*, the apostle formally develops enthymemic arguments from 9:7. Equally the *peroratio* cannot begin as early as 10:18; if anything it comprises only 10:31-11:1.

It has long been recognized that 1 Corinthians is made up of discrete subject units. The reason is that Paul is not in control of his subject matter; throughout the letter he is reacting to two very different sets of data, one emanating from Chloe's people (1 Cor 1:11), the other listed in the letter from Corinth (1 Cor 7:1). What he says is dictated by the diverse needs of the community. Inevitably one has the impression of a lack of unity, but a variety of subjects does not necessarily mean a multiplicity of letters. The opposite is suggested by *QFr* 3, in which Cicero replies point by point to five letters from his brother Quintus. In consequence, his letter is much longer than usual and the thought more dispersed, but no one has postulated a series of different letters. Neither is it necessary in the case of 1 Corinthians.

THE IMPORTANCE OF THE *PROPOSITIO*

The methodology latent in the above rhetorical analyses of the Pauline letters needs to be made explicit because it highlights their fragility. The starting point is the assumption that Paul follows the rhetorical schema. This is initially confirmed by the fact that the thanksgiving discussed above (p. 62) fulfils the same function as the *exordium*. Then the text of the epistle is divided in such a way as to correspond to the successive parts of the schema.

It is at this point that the rhetorical approach as it is currently practiced becomes problematic. The division is controlled by what one expects to find. None of the authors cited have developed any controls to reduce the danger of misinterpretations of both Paul and the rhetorical theorists. On the one hand, the desire to find something in Paul which may be categorized according to the parts of the schema may lead to a distortion of his perspective; for example, a minor dimension of a section can be given an importance that it did not have in the apostle's intention. On the other hand, if Paul interpreted correctly does not fit with the normal definition of the proposed part of the schema, there is the tendency to seek incidental remarks in the rhetorical theorists which might justify the exception, forgetting what the theorists have said about the need for flexibility.

Discussing the arrangement (*dispositio*) of the argument the *Rhetorica ad Herennium* says:

> There are two types of layouts, one based on the rules of oratory, the other adapted to circumstances. A discourse is constructed according to the rules if the principles laid down in Book I are followed: *exordium, narratio, partitio, confirmatio, refutatio, peroratio.* . . . When it is necessary to bypass the rules, the layout is left to the judgement of the orator, who adapts it to the circumstances. It is possible to begin with the *narratio,* or by a solid proof, or by reading a document. It is

possible to put the *confirmatio* after the *exordium,* and to have
the latter followed by the *narratio.* Any number of permuta-
tions are possible but they must be demanded by the circumstances (3:16; Caplan).

Hence one can never assume what the next rhetorical element is
going to be.

The above dangers can be avoided only if, as Standaert (1986,
80) and Aletti (1990, 9–12) have insisted, rhetorical analysis begins
by focusing on the *propositio,* that is, the author's statement of
what he wants to get across. "At the beginning of every proof
is a proposition" (Quintilian, *Institutio Oratoria* 4:4.1). It is the
thesis which the following *confirmatio* has to prove. The extension of the influence of the *propositio* is the only objective clue
to the limits of the material covered by the rhetorical schema.

Furthermore the objective of a speech or a letter is normally
achieved by the cumulative effect of a number of worked-out
points. Thus, one should not assume that a document contains
only one *propositio.* Quintilian, with the wisdom of experience,
points out:

> Propositions may be single, double or manifold: this is due to
> more than one reason. For several charges may be combined,
> as when Socrates was accused of corrupting the youth and of
> introducing new superstitions; while single propositions may
> be made up of a number of arguments, as for instance when
> Aeschines is accused of misconduct as an ambassador on the
> ground that he lied, failed to carry out his instructions, wasted
> time, and accepted bribes. . . . If propositions are put forward
> singly with the proofs appended, they will form several distinct
> propositions, if they are combined they fall under the head of
> partition (*Institutio Oratoria* 4:4.5-7; Butler).

What this means in practice can be illustrated from Romans
(Aletti 1992, 392). The general *propositio* governing the entire letter is to be found in 1:16-17. It is preceded by the *exordium* (1:1-
15), and followed by the *narratio* (1:18-32) and *confirmatio* (2:1-
15:13). Within the *confirmatio,* however, is a whole series of sub-

propositions which are the centers of minor applications of the rhetorical schema. One such subunit, for example, is 5:1-8:39, which comprises *exordium* (5:1-11), *narratio* (5:12-19), *propositio* (5:20-21), *confirmatio* (6:1-8:30), and *peroratio* (8:31-39). Such blocks of material interact dynamically with each other to create the unified thrust of the whole letter.

What has to be diligently sought in Romans is much more evident in 1 Corinthians, which does not contain an overarching *propositio*. In each section Paul had a specific point to make, and he needed to go about it in a systematic way which combined clarity and persuasiveness. The rhetorical schema was the tried and proven method of achieving such a goal, and so he instinctively adopted it. Paul's protestations of rhetorical inadequacy (1 Cor 2:1) can no longer be taken at face value (Forbes 1955). The advantage of recognizing the rhetorical cast of his thought is well illustrated by Standaert's (1983) analysis of 1 Corinthians 12-14 (see p. 81 above), because his postulated *digressio* is the most convincing explanation for the place of 1 Corinthians 13 in the discussion of spiritual gifts (so also but more obscurely Probst 1991, 331; against Mack 1990, 64-66). No longer is it possible to treat this chapter as having once enjoyed an independent existence (Sanders 1966, 181-87); it is integral to a carefully thought-out approach.

The value of rhetorical criticism focused essentially on the *propositio* is that it stimulates a renewed examination from a different perspective of the minute articulation of Paul's thought. As such it cannot fail to illuminate the text of the letters. The dangers are that the letters may be tortured to fit on a Procrustean bed of oratorical theory, and that time is wasted on endless discussions of the precise definition of categories and their subdivisions. As Quintilian said, "this affectation of subtlety in the invention of technical terms is mere laborious ostentation" (3:9.21).

The flexibility on which the *Rhetorica ad Herennium* insists is complemented by the warning of Quintilian against ascribing "talismanic value to the arbitrary decrees of [rhetorical] theorists" (2:13.15). His words still retain their urgency and can serve as a fitting conclusion to this section:

Let no one however demand of me a rigid code of rules such as most authors of textbooks have laid down, or ask me to impose on students of rhetoric a system of laws as immutable as fate, a system in which injunctions as to the *exordium* and its nature lead the way; then come the *statement of facts* and the laws to be observed in this connexion: next the *proposition* or, as some prefer, the *digression*, followed by prescriptions as to the order in which the various questions should be discussed, with all the other rules, which some speakers follow as though they had no choice but to regard them as orders and as if it were a crime to take any other line.

If the whole of rhetoric could be thus embodied in one compact code, it would be an easy task of little compass. But most rules are liable to be altered by the nature of the case, circumstances of time and place, and by hard necessity itself. Consequently the all-important gift for an orator is a wise adaptability since he is called upon to meet the most varied emergencies. . . .

The rules of rhetoric have not the formal authority of laws or decrees of the plebs, but are, with all they contain, the children of expediency. I will not deny that it is generally expedient to conform to such rules, otherwise I would not be writing now. But if our friend expediency suggests some other course to us, why, we shall disregard the authority of the professors and follow her (*Institutio Oratoria* 2:13.1-7; Butler).

Chiasm and Concentric Composition

One final aspect of the formal structure of a Pauline letter needs to be considered, namely, concentric composition, in which the elements of a text are distributed symmetrically around a central point in such a way that the second half is inverted and balanced against the first. In other words, ideas or terms introduced in the order A-B-C are repeated in the reverse order C'-B'-A'.

The phenomenon, it is claimed, appears on two levels, that of whole letters and that of sections within letters. The former is illustrated by Bligh's (1969, 39) analysis of Galatians:

A. Prologue (1:1-12)
  B. Autobiographical Section (1:13-2:10)
    C. Justification by Faith (2:11-3:4)
      D. Arguments from Scripture (3:5-29)
        E. Central Chiasm (4:1-10)
      D'. Arguments from Scripture (4:11-31)
    C'. Justification by Faith (5:1-10)
  B'. Moral Section (5:11-6:11)
A'. Epilogue (6:12-18).

The latter is exemplified by Welch (1981a, 214) in a presentation of Galatians 4:1-7, which manifestly differs from that of Bligh (1969, 330) insofar as it does not account for the same number of verses:

A. The *heir* remains a *child* and *servant* (4:1)
  B. Until the time appointed of the *father* (4:2)
    C. When that time came, *God* sent forth his *Son* (4:4)
      D. Made under the *law* (4:4)
      D'. To redeem those under the *law* (4:5)
    C'. *God* sent forth the spirit of his *Son* (4:6)
  B'. That you cry, Abba, *Father* (4:6)
A'. That you are no more a *servant* but a *son* and *heir* (4:7)

Before examining the validity and consequence of such analyses, we must first ask to what extent they are rooted in the rhetorical tradition. To say the least, the situation is somewhat obscure. Claims have been made that the *Iliad* of Homer, the *Shield of Heracles* by Hesiod, the *History* of Herodotus, and Plato's *Republic* are all constructed on this concentric pattern (Lohr 1961, 425). Were such the case, however, one would expect the rhetorical theorists to have discussed the technique and given rules for its application.

The quest for such evidence has produced very meager results. Standaert (1978, 36) gives prominence only to Plato's dictum:

> Every speech should be constructed like a living being. It should have a body and not lack head or feet. It should have a middle and two ends, which should be so formulated as to relate to each other and the whole (*Phaedo* 264C).

The banality of this assertion is not removed by the recommendation of a certain correspondence between the beginning and end of a discourse, because it does not say what kind of correspondence it should be. The *Rhetorica ad Herennium* is rather more practical in its advice.

> In the Proof and Refutation of arguments it is appropriate to adopt an Arrangement of the following sort: (1) the strongest arguments should be placed at the beginning and end of the pleading; (2) those of medium force, and also those that are neither useless to the discourse nor essential to the proof, which are weak if presented separately and individually, but become strong and plausible when conjoined with others should be placed in the middle (3:10.18; Caplan).

Quintilian terms this arrangement "Homeric" (*Institutio Oratoria* 5:12.14), because of Homer's description of the battle dispositions on the plain before Troy.

> Nestor put his charioteers with their horses and cars in the front; and at the back a mass of first-rate infantry to serve as rearguard. In between, he stationed his inferior troops, so that even shirkers would be forced to fight (*Iliad* 4:299; Rieu).

Such a structure is entirely consistent with the rhetorical principle that a speech should end, not with a whimper, but with a bang. Quintilian insisted, "we should avoid descending from the strongest proofs to the weakest" (*Institutio Oratoria* 5:12.14).

Concentrically Structured Documents

It should be evident that none of these texts furnish any theoretical basis for the sort of detailed concentric organization which Bligh has postulated for Galatians, and which Welch (1981a) also claims is the principle of organization of 1 Corinthians (216–17), Ephesians (221–22), Philemon (225–26), 1 Timothy (226–27) and 2 Timothy (229–30). On the contrary, the texts cited contradict the key assumption of Welch's analysis (to which many others also subscribe), namely, that the function of a concentric arrangement is to create "framing passages leading up to or away from each central statement" (1981a, 225). The structure, in other words, is designed to highlight what the author wants to emphasize. In classical rhetoric, however, the center is always the weakest point! Further evidence of the implausibility of Welch's position becomes manifest when we ask whether the center he distinguishes is in fact the key element of any given letter. Since space prohibits a complete analysis, two examples must suffice. The center of 1 Corinthians, he claims, comprises chapters 5–11. Are the variety of problems considered in these chapters really more significant in Paul's mind than the denial of the resurrection with which he deals in chapter 15? The answer, of course, is negative. It should be obvious that 1 Corinthians does not have a center insofar as it deals with a series of issues which are not intrinsically related. Welch considers 4:1-6 the center of Ephesians, but entitles it "Interlude"! He fails to convince because these verses are not even a complete literary unit, being merely the first portion of the opening of the second half of the letter (4:1-16).

In order to create an overarching concentric arrangement for a complete document one has to understand and classify the component parts in such a way as to emphasize the matching pairs. A certain degree of generalization is obviously necessary. The critical question concerns the point at which the specific meaning of a section is lost to a generic title; when this happens the procedure becomes illegitimate.

In order to illustrate the unlimited scope the concentric approach offers for subjective eisegesis, let us look at Bligh's justification for matching B (Gal 1:13–2:10) and B' (Gal 5:11–6:11).

> The correspondence between the Autobiographical Section and the Moral Section is not immediately obvious; but, as will be shown in the appropriate section of the commentary, the Moral Section is a description of the Two Ways of living, or rather, of the Way of Life and the Way of Death, here called "walking according to the Spirit" and "walking according to the flesh." If, then, St. Paul means this passage to be compared with 1:13-2:10, he must have intended the Autobiographical Passage to demonstrate that before his conversion he walked according to the flesh, and since his conversion, whatever his adversaries may say, he has walked according to the Spirit. This

> [concentric] structure of the Epistle suggests, therefore, that the
> main purpose of the Autobiographical Passage is not, as has
> often been supposed, to prove by an elaborate alibi that Paul
> did not receive the gospel from the other apostles, but rather
> to show that throughout his Christian life he has been obeying
> the promptings of the Holy Spirit (39–40).

Not only has Bligh assumed a correspondence which does not
exist, but in order to create it he completely distorts the meaning
of 1:13–2:10. The fact that Paul felt obliged to account here for
every moment of his time since his conversion indicates that he
was in fact constructing an alibi, and not merely affirming his
obedience to the Spirit.

The search for concentric structures covering a complete letter
has little to recommend it. Such an arrangement has no basis in
the rhetorical tradition. The approach necessarily involves gener-
alizations which become progressively more subjective as they approach higher degrees of abstraction. Finally, the analyses
published so far signally fail to carry conviction. It is significant
that Nils Lund, the pioneer of this form of research, who was
accused by Jeremias (1958, 145) of trying to account for over-
large blocks of text, never postulated a chiastic structure for an
entire document.

Concentrically Structured Parts of Documents

The situation is completely different with regard to parts within
a letter. Often inaccurately applied to extended concentric structures, the term *chiasm* is perfectly appropriate here. The word
is a transcription of the Greek *chiasma* which means "the diagonal
arrangement, especially of the clauses of a period so that the 1st
corresponds with the 4th and the 2nd with the 3rd" (LSJ, 1991b).
The Greek letter *chi* is written *X*.

On the simplest level this structure is common in all written
cultures from the second millennium, when slaves mocked their
masters' lack of practical skills (Smith 1981, 17).

> Like a LORD build—like a *slave* live;
> $\updownarrow$
> Like a *slave* build—like a LORD live.

through the New Testament period,

> The SABBATH was made for *man*;
> ↕
> Not *man* for the SABBATH (Mk 2:27).

right up to the present day,

> OLD KING COLE was *a merry old soul*
> ↕
> And a *merry old soul* was HE.

Similar examples in Paul are not difficult to find:

> Tongues are a sign not for BELIEVERS but for *unbelievers;*
> ↕
> But prophecy is not for *unbelievers* but for BELIEVERS (1 Cor 14:22).

> He who was called in the Lord as a SLAVE is a *freedman* of the Lord;
> ↕
> Likewise he who was *free* when called is a SLAVE of Christ (1 Cor 7:22).

Such antitheses are easily expanded, and not difficult to create. In the latter instance the principle is enunciated first (7:20), then chiastically developed (7:21-23), and closes with a repetition of the principle (7:24):

> A. Everyone should remain in the state in which he was called:
> B. Were you a SLAVE when you were called. Never mind. Yet if you can become free, make use of the opportunity.
> C. For he who was called in the Lord as a SLAVE is a *freedman* of the Lord.
> C'. Likewise he who was *free* when called is a SLAVE of Christ.
> B'. You were brought with a price; do not become SLAVES of men.
> A'. Everyone, believers, should remain with God in the state in in which he was called.

The plausibility of this example is enhanced by the limited number of matching terms and by the unambiguous definition of its limits.

More complex arrangements, however, are also postulated. Welch's analysis of Galatians 4:1-7 has already been noted (see p. 87 above). Aletti (1991, 162) proposes the following structure for Romans 9:6-29, giving only the matching words:

A. (vv. 6-9)   Israel (v. 6b)—descendants (vv. 7-8)
  B. (vv. 10-13) to love (v. 13)
    C. (vv. 14-18)   to pity (vv. 15, 16, 18)
                       to will (vv. 16, 18)
                       power (v. 17)
                       to show (v. 17)

    C'. (vv. 19-23)   to will (v. 22)
                       to show (v. 22)
                       power (v. 22)
                       pity (v. 23)
  B'. (vv. 24-26)   to love (v. 25)
A'. (vv. 27-29)   Israel (v. 27)—descendants (v. 29)

In examples such as these the repetition of the same words or very close synonyms appears to guarantee a certain objectivity. The words when taken out of context reveal a pattern (but have all the terms been taken into consideration?), and the only alternative to conscious arrangement would seem to be the rather implausible postulate of random coincidence. Problems, however, increase in proportion to the complexity of the arrangement and the length of the passage in question. It is not without significance that a developed pattern is never evident at first sight. It is something that has to be worked out patiently. This carries a subtle danger. The satisfaction of having thrown light on a perfectly balanced formal arrangement dulls the critical sense of the discoverer. The symmetry of the pattern, one feels, has a value in itself. A thing of beauty is a joy forever; the mystery of its meaning is part of its bewitching charm.

Such formal analysis, however, is merely a tool, and we must ask what end it serves. What is the significance of the chiasm, and why does an author use it at one point and not at others?

An answer to the second question becomes imperative only if a satisfactory response can be given to the first.

At the simplest level there is no doubt that the chiasm is nothing but a minor rhetorical device used to avoid monotony. If the same words are used, their order at least should be varied. The wit inherent in such a play on words is recognized by the *Rhetorica ad Herennium* (4:39) and Quintilian (*Institutio Oratoria* 9:3.85), both of whom quote the same example, "I do not live to eat, but eat to live"; they give it no profound significance.

In consequence their silence regarding the more extensive usage of the figure discerned by New Testament commentators is all the more significant. It was not part of their tradition. New rules, therefore, have to be evolved to judge extended chiasms. Since the practitioners all give most importance to the central element framed by the matching parts of the text, it seems reasonable to make it the criterion. Is the central element in fact the key statement in the literary unit delimited by the concentric structure? It would be difficult, if not impossible, to provide a convincing affirmative answer as far as the vast majority of the published chiasms are concerned. If such is the case, what is the point of the concentric structure? And if it does not have a point, is the concentric structure intentional or merely a projection of the commentator?

The problem is beautifully illustrated by Aletti. The thrust of his concentric analysis of Romans 9:6-29 led to the conclusion that "the units C and C' constitute the point of the passage" (1991, 164). But when he analyzed the same passage a year later in traditional rhetorical terms, he concluded that 9:6a was the *propositio* commanding the following *confirmatio* (9:6b-29) which itself was divided into two *subpropositiones* (9:6b and 9:14), each followed by its appropriate justification. In the light of this careful analysis of Paul's thought and how it was expressed, he said of his concentric analysis that "in itself this chiastic arrangement does not reveal either the point at issue or the apostle's response" (1992, 389). I would extend this negative assessment to all concentric structures discerned in the Pauline letters.

This, however, leaves unanswered the question of whether the verbal repetition characteristic of the extended chiasm is intentional or not. A negative answer does not demand that we assume the creativity of coincidence. A middle road is indicated by a casual remark of Aletti. "In the Pauline letters a concentric or chiastic structure is often due to known rhetorical principles, according to which a concrete problem is first presented and discussed (A), then elaborated through comparison with others (B), before and with a view to a definitive solution (A')" (1992, 399). Since such is in fact the case, as we shall see in a moment, it is not surprising that Paul, who is not concerned to vary his terminology, should occasionally produce a concatenation of identical words at the beginning and end of a development. This means that the balanced structure, insofar as it really exists, was not a conscious goal but merely a by-product of the pattern of his thought. The plausibility of this solution is enhanced by the fact that it also explains why the structure appears only sporadically and in apparently arbitrary fashion.

Since the great commentary on 1 Corinthians (1910) by Johannes Weiss, it has been recognized that material in the Pauline letters is sometimes organized according to the pattern A—B—A' in which the apostle returns to the original topic after having apparently abandoned it. The postulated correspondence is exclusively on the thematic level, and no verbal similarities are invoked to justify it.

The most thorough effort to find examples of this arrangement is that of Brunot (1955, 41–51). He has little difficulty in furnishing convincing examples within letters, notably from 1 Corinthians.

A.	Fornication (5:1-13)	
B.	Lawsuits (6:1-11)	
A'.	Fornication (6:12-20)	

A.	Food Offered to Idols (8:1-13)	
B.	The Use of Freedom (9:1–10:13)	
A'.	Food Offered to Idols (10:14–11:1)	

A.	The Eucharist at Corinth (11:17-22)	
B.	The Institution of the Eucharist (11:23-26)	
A'.	The Eucharist at Corinth (11:27-34)	

A.	The Gifts of the Spirit (12)	
B.	Love (13)	
A'.	The Gifts of the Spirit (14)	

The characteristic feature of this arrangement is a shift from one subject to another and then back to the original topic. Various explanations are possible. An inept editor could be made responsible (Héring, 11). It might be thought to be an accident due to distraction, as if Paul carelessly followed an errant thought and only later realized that he had not finished what he intended to say. The frequent repetition of the pattern makes this hypothesis implausible, and a proper appreciation of the content makes the editor hypothesis both implausible and unnecessary. Close examination of each case shows that the "digression" is essential to the point that Paul is attempting to get across. Thus, for example, in 1 Corinthians 5–6 Paul's concern about the witness impact of immoral behavior (A and A') is clarified and reinforced by his insistence that the community should demonstrate to outsiders the reconciling force of love by solving its problems internally rather than having recourse to lawsuits (B).

Here once again, however, a valid insight can be pushed too far, as when the ABA' arrangement is asked to account for a whole letter. Brunot (1955, 44) considers this pattern to be the explanation of the organization of 2 Corinthians:

A.   Paul's Apology and Apostolic Ministry (1–7)
B.   The Collection for Jerusalem (8–9)
A'. Paul's Apology (10–13)

Not only does this proposal signally fail to account for the subtlety of this highly complex letter, but it ignores the well-founded arguments that chapters 10–13 cannot have belonged to the same letter as chapters 1–9 (Murphy-O'Connor 1991a, 10–12). The proposed structure has as little to do with Paul's intention as the present form of 2 Corinthians.

Epistolary Classification of Letters

Since letters were such an important part of daily life throughout the whole spectrum of society, it was inevitable that there should be aids to composition. Unfortunately only two such manuals have survived.

The oldest is the *Typoi Epistolikoi* (Weichert 1910; Malherbe 1977) erroneously attributed to Demetrius of Phalerum (b. ca.

350 B.C.). The proposed dates range between 200 B.C. and A.D. 300, but it is almost certain that it was in existence before A.D. 100. It is referred to as Pseudo-Demetrius. This work is not to be confused with the *Peri Hermēneias* (On Style), which also touches on the epistolary art, and which was also attributed to Demetrius of Phalerum; it possibly was written by Demetrius of Tarsus in the late first century B.C. The authorship of the second manual is no more secure. The *Epistolimaioi Charactēres* (Weichert 1910; Malherbe 1977) is associated with the name of Libanius or Proclus and is dated sometime between A.D. 300 and 600. It is referred to as Pseudo-Libanius.

Pseudo-Demetrius divides letters into twenty-one types whereas Pseudo-Libanius discusses forty-one styles of letters. Note that style has nothing to do with the quality of writing, and type does not imply the sort of detailed theoretical treatment that we encountered in the discussion of rhetorical forms. What is meant is best illustrated by an example. Both authors deal with the problem of a letter conveying displeasure.

Pseudo-Demetrius

The blaming type [of letter] is one that undertakes not to seem to be too harsh.

Since time has not yet permitted you to return thanks for the favors you have received, (your failure to do so) is not the reason why I supposed it well not to mention what you have received. And yet you will (continue to) be annoyed with us, and impute words (to us). We do, then, blame you for having such a disposition, and we blame ourselves for not knowing that you are such a man (4:5–11; Malherbe 1977, 31).

Pseudo-Libanius

The blaming kind [of letter] is that in which we blame someone.

The blaming letter. You did not act well when you wronged those who did good to you. For by insulting your benefactors, you provided an example of evil to others (15:17–16.1; 22.4–6; Malherbe 1977, 71).

These are typical of the way the two manuals are organized. The kind of letter is first defined and then illustrated by means of a specimen (for other illustrations see Stowers 1986, 58–60). The example, however, is never a complete letter designed to be adapted by the writer, but always a suggestive indication of how an appropriate mood should be conveyed in writing (Koskenniemi 1956, 62). It responds to the question "How should I go about this?" of someone capable of acting on a hint, rather than to the question "What exactly should I say and in what order?" of a person who needs to have everything spelt out in detail.

In order to see how the Pauline letters would fare in this sort of classification, it will be helpful to have the list of the twenty-one types of letter identified by Pseudo-Demetrius (White 1986, 203):

Friendly (*philikos*)

Commendatory (*systatikos*)	Blaming (*memptikos*)
Reproachful (*oneidistikos*)	Consoling (*paramythētikos*)
Censorius (*epitimētikos*)	Admonishing (*nouthetētikos*)
Threatening (*apeilētikos*)	Vituperative (*psektikos*)
Praising (*epainetikos*)	Advisory (*symbouleutikos*)
Supplicatory (*axiēmatikos*)	Inquiring (*erōtēmatikos*)
Responding (*apophantikos*)	Allegorical (*allēgorikos*)
Accounting (*aitiologikos*)	Accusing (*katēgorikos*)
Apologetic (*apologētikos*)	Congratulatory (*sugcharētikos*)
Ironic (*eirōnikos*)	Thankful (*apeucharistikos*)

This list is no more exhaustive than the categories are exclusive or their names unique. The list of Pseudo-Libanius is twice as long, and his last category he calls "mixed" (*miktē*) because in many cases the writer may need to do a number of different things in the same letter, for example, to blame some aspects of a family member's behavior while praising others.

In the process of illustrating these various types by letters drawn from pagan and Christian antiquity, Stowers (1987, 96, 97, 109, 114, 128, 134, 155, 156) incidentally classifies the Pauline letters as follows:[5]

Rom:	Mixed, essentially protreptic but with a commendatory conclusion
1 Cor:	Mixed, paraenetic and advisory

2 Cor:	Mixed, hortatory, advisory, blaming, threatening, accusing.
Gal:	Mixed, hortatory and advisory
Phil:	Mixed, paraenetic, commendatory, thankful
1 Thess:	Paraenetic
2 Thess:	Admonishing
Phlm:	Supplicatory
2 Tim:	Paraenetic

Aune (1987, 206–12), for his part, classifies 1 Thessalonians as paraenetic, Galatians as deliberative, Philippians as gratitude and paraenesis, and Philemon as recommendation.

The schematic character of these characterizations should be evident to anyone with even a rudimentary knowledge of the Pauline letters. No one category can do justice to the complexity of a Pauline epistle. Virtually all Pseudo-Demetrius⁵ types are to be found in every letter. In consequence, the value of epistolary classification of whole letters must be considered extremely dubious. Where the traditional categories might prove useful is in classifying parts of various letters with a view to comparison.

Conclusion

The key word in the conclusion of the ordinary Greek letter is *errōso* if there is only one recipient, and *errōsthe* if the recipients are multiple. They are the singular and plural perfect imperative passive of *rōnnymi* "to strengthen, make strong." Hence literally, "Be made strong," or more elegantly, "Farewell." The Latin equivalent is *Vale/Valete*. It was often associated with other elements, for example, a wish for the health of the recipient, a request for the recipient to greet others, greetings from those with the sender, the date. The following illustrations are all from the first century A.D.

---

⁵ He uses "*protreptic* in reference to hortatory literature that calls the audience to a new and different way of life, and *paraenesis* for advice and exhortation to continue in a certain way of life" (92).

Therefore if it meets with your approval, you will make an effort to assist him, as is right. For the rest, take care to stay well. Farewell. Year 3 of Tiberius Caesar Augustus, Phaophi 3 (*POxy* IV, 746; White 1986, 118).

Get all the grain in the granary moved because of the inundation. Farewell. Salute Thermion and your children. Year 5, Soter 21 (*PRyl* II, 231; White 1986, 123).

Indike to her lady Thaisous. Greeting. I send the breadbasket to you by means of Taurinos, the camel driver; regarding which please send word to me that you received it. Salute my lord Theon and Nikoboulos and Dioskopos and Theon and Hermokles, may all be free from harm. Longinus salutes you. The month Germanic (. . .) 2. (*POxy* II, 300; White 1986, 146).

In the New Testament the conventional Greek *errōso/errōsthe* appears only in the two letters in the Acts, that of the Jerusalem conference (15:29), and that of Claudius Lyias to the governor Felix (23:30—missing in the better manuscripts).

Despite significant variety in length, style, and content, the conclusions to Paul's letters exhibit a consistent pattern which Gamble (1977, 83) has defined as follows:

> Hortatory Remarks
> Wish of Peace
> Greetings
>   Greeting with the kiss
> Grace-Benediction

These elements will be dealt with in reverse order, leaving out the hortatory remarks, which are the most amorphous and the least susceptible to formal analysis.

The Final Blessing

The concluding benediction is as consistent in form as the opening greeting to which it is related by the emphasis on "grace." The "peace" component of the opening greeting becomes an independent element in the conclusion.

Rom:	The grace of our Lord Jesus Christ be with you.
1 Cor:	The grace of the Lord Jesus be with you. My love be with you all in Christ Jesus. Amen.
2 Cor:	The grace of the Lord Jesus Christ and the love of God and the fellowship of the Holy Spirit be with you all.
Gal:	The grace of our Lord Jesus Christ be with your spirit. Amen.
Eph:	Grace be with all who love our Lord Jesus Christ with love undying.
Phil:	The grace of the Lord Jesus Christ be with your spirit.
Col:	Grace be with you.
1 Thess:	The grace of our Lord Jesus Christ be with you.
2 Thess:	The grace of our Lord Jesus Christ be with you all.
1 Tim:	Grace be with you.
2 Tim:	The Lord be with your spirit. Grace be with you.
Titus:	Grace be with you all.
Phlm:	The grace of the Lord Jesus Christ be with your spirit.

The consistent formula in the opening greeting is "grace to you . . . from" and the source of that grace is first God the Father and only then the Lord Jesus Christ (see p. 53 above). Here, on the contrary, the basic formula is "grace with you" and the grace is specified as that of the Lord Jesus Christ. The genitive in this latter case is a genitive of origin (BDF §162), which makes it the equivalent of "from" in the opening greeting. Jesus Christ is the mediator of grace because God has made him Lord (Phil 2:9-11). The ultimate source of grace, therefore, is always God. Here, however, the emphasis is on its incarnation in history in the person of Jesus Christ, who is "the power of God" (1 Cor 1:24). Paul's wish is that his readers should be empowered to display in their comportment "the life of Jesus" (2 Cor 4:10-11), that is, a lifestyle committed to the love of others unto the ultimate sacrifice.

The original formula, "The grace of our Lord Jesus Christ be with you/your spirit" (1 Thess 5:28; 2 Thess 3:18; Gal 6:18; Phil 4:23; Phlm 25; in Rom 16:20 it is not the last verse) is supplemented in 1 Corinthians by "My love be with you all in Christ Jesus. Amen" (16:23-24), whereas in 2 Corinthians it is expanded into "The grace of our Lord Jesus Christ and the love of God and the fellowship of the Holy Spirit be with you all" (13:14). Ephesians is even more developed and curiously contains the two elements of the opening greeting, "Peace be to the believers and love with faith from God the Father and the Lord Jesus Christ. Grace be with all who love our Lord Jesus Christ with love undying" (6:23-24). In striking contrast is the brevity of "Grace be with you" (Col 4:18; 1 Tim 6:21; 2 Tim 4:22; Titus 3:15), which in 2 Timothy is preceded by "The Lord be with your spirit."

Apropos of the more developed forms one can only hypothesize that the solemnity of the blessing in 2 Corinthians is designed as somewhat belated compensation for the tone of 2 Corinthians [10-13 (so rightly Plummer 1915, 383)]. Though not in any way Trinitarian in Paul's mind, his formulation together with others (e.g., 1 Pet 1:1) fostered the theological speculation which eventually became a credal formulation (Barrett 1973, 345).

In terms of those addressed the only variation in the standard formula is the alternation of "with you (all)" (1 and 2 Thess, Rom, 1 and 2 Cor, Eph) and *meta tou pneumatos hymōn*, "with your [pl.] spirit [sing.] (Gal, Phil, Phlm). The commentators state only the obvious, namely, that there is no difference in meaning. Why then the change in formulation? The consistency of the form of the greeting indicates that it was not simply for the sake of variety. It is possible that in Galatians the use of "your spirit" was suggested by the reference to "my body" in the previous verse, but nothing similar appears in Philippians and Philemon.

The concluding doxology of Romans (16:25-27) is a special problem. Even though it is firmly attested in the manuscripts, its authenticity has been questioned on internal grounds. Considerations of content, style, and epistolary practice conspire to make it unlikely that Paul was the author (Elliott 1981; Dunn 1988, 913-16). He does not end letters in this way. The absence of any mention of Christ in "the revelation of the mystery concealed for long ages, but now made manifest through the prophetic scriptures" (16:25b–26a) betrays its un-Pauline character, even though its language evokes that of Colossians 1:26-27 and Ephesians 3:4-6.

Greetings

Greetings are a regular feature of Pauline letters (Mullins 1968). The verb is always *aspazomai*, "to greet," as in the papyrus letters, but inevitably the wide range of Paul's contacts is reflected in the variety of formulations.

Rom: (Paul greets twenty-six individuals and five groups and continues:) Greet one another with a holy kiss. All the churches of Christ greet you (16:3-16).
Timothy, my fellow-worker, greets you; so do Lucius, and Jason, and Sosipater, my kinsmen. I, Tertius, the writer of this letter, greet you in the Lord. Gaius, who is host to me and to the whole church, greets you. Erastus, the city treasurer, and our brother Quartus, greet you (16:21-24).

1 Cor: The churches of Asia send greetings. Aquila and Prisca and the church in their house send you hearty greetings in the Lord. All the believers send greetings. Greet one another with a holy kiss (16:19-20).

2 Cor: Greet one another with a holy kiss. All the saints greet you (13:13).

Gal:

Eph:

Phil: The believers who are with me greet you. All the saints greet you, especially those of Caesar's household (4:21b-22).

Col: Aristarchus my fellow prisoner greets you, and Mark . . . and Jesus who is called Justus. . . . Epaphras, who is one of yourselves, a servant of Christ Jesus, greets you, always remembering you earnestly in his prayers. . . . Luke the beloved physician and Demas greet you. Give my greetings to the believers at Laodicea and to Nympha and the church in her house (4:10-15).

1 Thess: Greet all the believers with a holy kiss.

2 Thess:

1 Tim:

2 Tim: Greet Prisca and Aquila, and the household of Onesiphorus. . . . Eubulus sends greetings to you, as do Pudens, and Linus and Claudia and all the believers (4:19-21).

Titus: All who are with me send greetings to you. Greet those who love us in the faith (3:15).

Phlm: Epaphras, my fellow prisoner in Christ, sends greetings to you, and so do Mark, Aristarchus, Demas, and Luke, my fellow-workers (23-24).

At first sight the absence of any greeting in Galatians and 2 Thessalonians is surprising, but on reflection it becomes easy to explain; in both letters Paul is too preoccupied for pleasantries. Both communities have disappointed him, and all his attention is focused on being properly understood. Moreover, a certain stiffness on his part should have a sobering effect on his readers.

Greetings would be out of place in a general letter such as Ephesians, not only because of the increased length, but also because the members of one church would not necessarily know those of others. Moreover, the presence of names would have complicated the process of copying the letter.

The silence of 1 Timothy is an indication of its artificiality. The contrast with the warmth of the greetings in 2 Timothy is striking and constitutes another argument against the authenticity of 1 Timothy.

The Position of the Greeting

Predominantly the greetings come immediately before the final blessing. Such is the case with 2 Corinthians, Philippians, Colossians, 2 Timothy, Titus, and Philemon. Those in Colossians and

2 Timothy are briefly interrupted by an injunction, which in 1 Thessalonians separates the greeting from the final blessing.

Romans 16:21-23 is the only greeting to come after the final blessing. Given the extended list of those greeted in 16:3-16, it is manifestly an afterthought. The explanation is probably very simple. Noticing that the last page had not been completely filled, Timothy requested that his greetings be transmitted, and others followed suit. Only because of this do we know the name of one of Paul's secretaries, Tertius. It is only such accidents that give us occasional faint glimpses of the interaction of the group around Paul.

In 1 Corinthians the greeting exceptionally occurs before the personal postscript. The explanation is probably to be found in the nature of the letter. On one level it is an official response to a letter from the church of Corinth (7:1), and it concludes with advice concerning the administration of the community there (16:15-18). Writing from Ephesus (16:8), the capital of Asia, in an official mode, Paul thought it appropriate to send greetings from the churches of that province, which he also supervised. The decision may have been no more than a simple reflex, but on reflection he would immediately see that it could function as another hint to the Corinthians that they were not the only Christians (1:2).

The Source of the Greeting

In three letters Paul identifies himself as the source; in each case the formula is identical, *Ho aspasmos tē emē cheiri Paulou* (2 Thess 3:17; 1 Cor 16:21; Col 4:18). The literal rendering is "The greeting in my hand of Paul" and it has given rise to the idea that the greeting must be outside this clause (Roller 1933, 165–66). Manifestly, however, the genitive stands in apposition to the dative; the greeting of Paul is written in his own hand.

Another formulation also lends itself to misunderstanding. In Thessalonians 5:26 and Philippians 4:21 Paul uses the imperative *aspasasthe,* "greet." When this same imperative appears in Colossians 4:15; 2 Timothy 4:19; and Titus 3:15 it is clear from the context that those whom he salutes are distinct from the recipients of the letters. Thus it could be thought that the Thessalonians or Philippians were to pass on his greetings to "every saint in Christ Jesus," meaning other believers who did not belong to the community. In Pauline terms this is a contradiction (Murphy-O'Connor 1982, 175–86). It is ridiculous to imagine that Paul is thinking in terms of the occasional Christian who might pass through Philippi. Clearly he is saluting the whole community to which the letter is addressed and so the phrase should be translated, "I greet every saint in Christ Jesus." One cannot assume, as Gnilka does (1968, 181) that the command is addressed to the "supervisors and assistants" (Phil 1:1) who will then transmit Paul's greetings to the rest of the community. Confirmation is furnished by the fact that he then mentions the greetings of "those with me" and finally the greetings of "those of the household of Caesar"; the greeters form an ever-widening circle. The same interpretation must be given to the same imperative in Romans 16:3 (so rightly Gamble 1977, 93), which Dunn (1988, 891) aptly paraphrases, "Greetings to. . . ."

In 1 Thessalonians the greeting originates with Paul and his coauthors. Elsewhere the source of the greeting is those with Paul, who desire to be remembered to the recipients or whom Paul thinks would like to be mentioned.

The most complex greeting is that of 1 Corinthians, where there are three sources: (1) the churches of Asia, (2) Aquila and Prisca and their house church, (3) all the believers. The order is intriguing. I suspect that it was Paul's intention to mention only the churches of the province of Asia, for the reason given above. The abrupt shift from this impersonal level to the intimate level of his close friends suggests that it was Aquila and/or Prisca who asked to be mentioned, because of their close connection with the Corinthians (cf. Acts 18:1-3). The mention of their house church in turn stimulated Paul to include a reference to "all the believers," that is, the "whole" Church (1 Cor 14:23).

In addition to Philippians (see above), the source of the greeting in two letters is generic and the tone rather formal, "all the saints" (2 Cor), "those with me" (Titus). The artificiality of Titus as an imitation of a Pauline letter explains its stiffness. The mood of bitter disappointment which animates 2 Corinthians 10–13 must have been shared by Paul's companions, who in consequence would have had little interest in sending good wishes.

The reserve of Philippians is more difficult to explain, because Paul's relations with the community were excellent. It may be related to the embarrassment which tinges the expression of his gratitude for the money the Philippians had sent him (4:10-20). There was a certain danger in being in receipt of a personal gift at the precise moment when he was trying to persuade churches to participate in the collection for the poor of Jerusalem. His enemies could claim that he was lining his own pocket (2 Cor 12:14).

In another series the greeters are named, eight in Romans, five each in Colossians and Philemon, and four plus "all the believers" in 2 Timothy. These reflect much more normal situations in which affection surges up between believers who may only have heard of one another. With regard to what was said above (p. 16) concerning coauthorship, it is important to note that the presence of such people with Paul when the letters were being written underlines that the choice of one or two to figure in the addresses was a matter of conscious strategy.

THE RECIPIENTS OF THE GREETING

As a general rule the recipients of the greetings are not named. It would have been invidious to single out individuals belonging to communities in which Paul knew everyone because he had lived and worked among them. Far from being an exception to this rule, Romans, which greets twenty-six individuals (all but two by name) and five groups, is unambiguous evidence that Paul was writing to a Church in which he had never ministered. Thus Romans 16 cannot have been at one stage an independent letter addressed to Ephesus, as some have argued (e.g., most recently, Refoulé). This conclusion is confirmed by Colossians, in which Paul singles out "the brethren at Laodicea and Nympha and the church in her house" (4:15). Paul was not the founder of the churches in the Lycus valley and had never visited them.

It is not necessary to assume that Paul personally met all the twenty-six individuals mentioned in Romans, but he definitely was acquainted with a certain number. Prisca and Aquila had been with him at Corinth (Acts 18:2) and later at Ephesus (1 Cor 16:19). The connotation of *agapētos mou* which qualifies Epaenetus, Ampilatus, and Stachys is well brought out by the paraphrase "my dear friend'' (NJB), which cannot be an empty formula; it implies an intimate relationship. If the mother of Rufus had also "mothered" Paul, he must have known both. An element of doubt clouds the case of Andronicus and Junia because "my fellow prisoners" might mean only that they had suffered imprisonment as Paul had done. In Colossians 4:10 and Philemon 23 the context indicates that Aristarchus and Epaphras were imprisoned with Paul, but such is not the case in Romans. That Paul should have known a minimum of seven and a maximum of nine who had moved from the east to Rome is well within the bounds of possibility.

Whence did he learn the names and praiseworthy achievements (Harnack 1928) of the others? Aquila and Prisca may have stayed in touch with Paul. Tertius, the secretary who wrote Romans (16:22), may have spent some time in Rome (Dunn 1988, 909). Or Paul may have instructed him to find out the names of some members of the Church at Rome. This function of a secretary is illustrated by Cicero, *Att* 4:5, in which he thanks Atticus for work done in his library, and by a second letter the same day in which the workers are named (*Att* 4:8), evidently after he had inquiries made and found out who they were (Richards 1991, 116, 171). Finally, it should not be forgotten that Paul had wanted to visit Rome for a long time (Rom 1:13; 15:22); his interest must have been stimulated by information, and curiosity would gather more.

Recipients of greetings are also named in 2 Timothy where Paul salutes "Prisca and Aquila, and the household of Onesiphorus" (4:19). In counter-distinction to all the other letters which are addressed to communities, this is addressed to a private individual who, moreover, was Paul's oldest and closest collaborator. In consequence, there was nothing to prevent him singling out certain individuals with whom he had a special relationship. This was certainly true of Prisca and Aquila, who had worked with him in Corinth and Ephesus. Onesiphorus had helped Paul when the latter was a prisoner in Rome (2 Tim 1:16); he and his family figure prominently in the *Acts of Paul* 2.

GREETING WITH THE KISS

The request that the recipients salute one another with "a holy kiss" (*philēma hagion*) is a less regular element in the greeting, being found in only four letters. This form of greeting must be distinguished from those initiated or transmitted by Paul, and is specifically Christian. The earliest formula is "Greet all the believers with a holy kiss" (1 Thess 5:26) which subsequently becomes "Greet one another with a holy kiss" (1 Cor 16:20; 2 Cor 13:12; Rom 16:16).

No explanations have been put forward for the apparently random way Paul uses what is obviously a fixed formula. All discussion has been sidetracked by the presence of a kiss as an element in liturgies of the second century and subsequently (Justin, *Apol,* 1.65; *Const Apol,* 2.57.12; 8.5.5; Hofmann). This gave rise to the hypothesis that in the letters the exchange of the kiss was intended as preparation for the celebration of the Eucharist which followed the public reading of the letter (e.g., J.A.T. Robinson 1962, 154–57). Recognition that the kiss served as a normal form of greeting both among Jews and Gentiles (cf. Luke 7:45; 15:20; 22:48; TDNT 9:119–27) has led to the dismissal of this hypothesis as unnecessarily specific (Gamble 1977, 75–76; Dunn 1988, 899).

The exchange of kisses among the members of a community symbolizes the unity of the group. It is an appropriate directive where there are tensions within a Church. This was certainly the case at Corinth where believers were divided on many issues (1 Cor 1:11-12). At Rome it is very likely that there were certain tensions between Jewish and Gentile Christians. It is not at all as clear that this type of situation existed at Thessalonica (1 Thess 4:1; 5:11). There may have been tension between those who continued to work and those who refused to (1 Thess 4:11) but then the lack of the directive to kiss one another in 2 Thessalonians is inexplicable, because the problem is there explicit (3:6-13).

The directive would be meaningless in the Pastorals and out of place in Galatians, where the community was unified in its opposition to Paul. There had been a split in the Colossian Church, but the letter is addressed only to those who remained faithful. Hence the directive was unnecessary, as in the cases of Ephesians,

Philippians and Philemon; in none of these communities is there any hint of division.

The Peace Wish

Rom:	The God of peace be with you. Amen (15:33).
1 Cor:	
2 Cor:	Live in peace and the God of love and peace will be with you (13:11).
Gal:	Peace and mercy be upon all who walk by this rule and on the Israel of God (6:16).
Eph:	Peace be to the believers, and love with faith, from God the Father and the Lord Jesus Christ (6:23).
Phil:	What you have learned and received and heard and seen in me, do; and the God of peace will be with you (4:9).
Col:	
1 Thess:	May the God of peace himself sanctify you wholly, and may your spirit and soul and body be kept sound and blameless at the coming of our Lord Jesus Christ (5:23).
2 Thess:	May the Lord of peace himself give you peace at all times in all ways. The Lord be with you all (3:16).
1 Tim:	
2 Tim:	
Titus:	
Phlm:	

It has already been noted that "peace from God" is a consistent element in the initial greeting of a Pauline letter. There it is always joined to "grace"; in the conclusion the two are regularly separated in the form of a wish that the Lord of peace (2 Thess 3:16) or the God of peace (1 Thess 5:23; 2 Cor 13:11; Phil 4:9; Rom 15:33; 16:20) may be with them (never with their "spirit" as in the final blessing) or accord various benefits. Peace is the direct object of the wish in Galatians 6:16 and Ephesians 6:23.

No peace wish appears in 1 Corinthians, Colossians, Philemon, and the Pastorals. The latter four may demonstrate that it was not Paul's custom to use the formula in letters to individuals. The closest 1 Corinthians comes is "God is not a God of confusion but of peace" (1 Cor 14:33; cf. 7:15), but this is not a wish and it is too far from the end of the letter.[6] Momentary distraction is perhaps the best explanation of the omission.

Postscripts

G. Bahr distinguishes two types of postscripts. One is what we would normally understand by the term, additional material attached to a letter as an afterthought. The other he terms a "record," and it is illustrated by the following letter dated A.D. 54.

> Ammonius, son of Ammonius, to Tryphon, son of Dionysius, greeting.
>
> I agree that I have sold to you the weaver's loom belonging to me, measuring three weaver's cubits less two palms, and containing two rollers and two beams, and I acknowledge the receipt from you through the bank of Sarapion, son of Lochus, near the Serapeum at Oxyrhynchus, of the price of it agreed between us, namely 20 silver drachmae of the Imperial and Ptolemaic coinage; and that I will guarantee to you the sale with every guarantee, under penalty of payment to you of the price which I have received from you increased by half its amount, and of the damages. This note of hand is valid. The 14th year of Tiberius Claudius Caesar Augustus Germanicus Imperator, the 15th of the month Caesareus.
>
> I, AMMONIUS, SON OF AMMONIUS, HAVE SOLD THE LOOM, AND HAVE RECEIVED THE PRICE OF 20 DRACHMAE OF SILVER AND WILL GUARANTEE THE SALE AS AFORESAID. I, HERACLIDES, SON OF DIONYSIUS, WROTE FOR HIM AS HE WAS ILLITERATE (P. Oxy 264; Bahr 1968, 28).

The shift to small capitals indicates that the last paragraph was written by a different hand. In antiquity one's name alone was

---

[6] The same criticism does not apply to Phil 4:9, which is in fact the conclusion of one of the component letters (see p. 32 above).

not sufficient for the legality of a business document written by a scribe. The signer, or his agent (the case here), had to demonstrate understanding and acceptance of the content by summarizing it (Mitteis 1908, 1:304–5).

The normal type of postscript is recognizable not by a change of hand but by its position, either after the Farewell or in the margin, and is amusingly illustrated by a papyrus letter dated 154 B.C.

> Sarapion to his brothers, Ptolemy and Apollonius, greeting. If you are well (it would be excellent). I myself am well. I have contracted with the daughter of Hesperos and intend to marry her in the month Mesore. Please send half a chous of olive oil to me. I wrote to you in order that you may know. Farewell. (Year) 28, Epeiph 21.
>
> Come for the (wedding) day, Apollonios (*UPZ* I, 66; White 1986, 73).

Why Ptolemy was not also invited to the party remains a mystery! Other examples in papyrus letters are numerous. The letter from Apion to Epimachos, the beginning of which has been quoted above (p. 56), concludes with a postscript in the left margin in which two of his friends send greetings. Another young sailor, who had written to his mother while waiting for his assignment, had a different scribe add a postscript saying that he would be based at Misenum (White 1986, 160–62).

Even someone as well organized as Cicero employed the postscript (see p. 80 above). He wrote a letter to Atticus which concluded with a reference to Niceas. When he got back the final fair copy, Cicero added:

> This in my own hand [*hoc manu mea*]. By chance I was chatting to Nicias about scholars when the conversation turned to Talna. According to Nicias there's nothing much to be said about his intelligence; a modest and careful man. One point, however, did not please me. Nicias assured me that he had reason to know that he recently made a proposal to Cornificia, the daughter of Quintus, who is no chicken and has been married many times. The women turned him down when they discovered that he had only 800,000 sesterces. I think you should look into it (*Att* 13:28.4–13:29.1).

In Cicero's case, as Richards has perceptively noted (1991, 85), the explicit *hoc manu mea,* "in my own hand," is not always necessary. In September 51 B.C. Cicero was campaigning in southeastern Asia Minor and wrote one letter to Cato and three to Marcellus (*Fam* 15:3; 15:7–9). All four contain a formula begging for consideration and protection while absent; the words (*peto) me absentem diligas et defendas,* "(I beg) that in my absence you may love and defend me," are a constant. In the first three letters the formula is the last line of the letter. In the fourth, however, it is followed by the words:

> As for the reports that I have received about the Parthians, I thought that I ought not even now to make them the subject of a public dispatch, and that is the reason why in spite of our intimacy I did not wish to write to you, lest, when I had written to a consul, it might be supposed that I had written officially (*Fam* 15:9.3; Williams).

This is certainly a postscript occasioned by Cicero's fear that his omission of any mention of the Parthians (who were threatening Syria) might be misinterpreted (Richards 1991, 85).

Both types of postscripts are found in the Pauline corpus. In demonstrating Paul's employment of a secretary we have had occasion to evoke his explicit references to taking up the pen; the name "Paul" and the phrase "in my own hand" are constant elements (1 Cor 16:21; Gal 6:11; Col 4:18; 2 Thess 3:17; Phlm 19). I have argued that 1 Thessalonians 5:27-28 should also be considered an unsigned postscript. Not only does it parallel the authenticating postscript in 2 Thessalonians 3:17-18, but this is the only reasonable explanation for the sudden shift to the first person singular in *enorkizō,* "I adjure."

Earlier I also refused Richards' suggestion that 2 Corinthians 10–13 should be considered the postscript to 2 Corinthians 1–9. It is in fact a separate letter. Thus two postscripts should be sought, one in chapter 9 and another in chapter 13. When dealing with coauthorship, I suggested, on the basis of the first person singular and the parallel in tone with Galatians 6:11-18, that all of chapter 9 should be considered such a postscript. Second Corinthians 10–13, on the other hand, is essentially an "I" letter with "we" interruptions. Thus the presence of the first person singular in 13:11-14 does not prove it to be a postscript.

Romans 16:21-23 is certainly a postscript, but it is possible that it is a postscript to a postscript. Cicero provides a parallel to such a procedure. In a letter to his brother Quintus he says, "Just as I was in the act of folding this letter, there came letter-carriers from you and Caesar" (*QFr* 3:1.17; Williams). He deals with that matter and then says, "After I had written these last words, which are in my own hand, your son Cicero came in and had dinner with me" (3.1.19). He reports on that visit saying, "I dictated this to Tiro during dinner, so do not be surprised at its being written in a different hand" (3.1.19), and the letter continues for five more long paragraphs!

Even though the Romans did not know Paul's handwriting, they would have expected a shift in script at the end of the letter (written by Tertius, 16:22) simply because it was conventional. The obvious candidate for the personal postscript is 16:17-20, which follows the long list of greetings, but the only argument for this hypothesis is that it ends with the stereotypical blessing, which appears in the autograph sections of 1 and 2 Thessalonians, 1 Corinthians, Galatians, and Philemon.

The same final blessing appears in Philippians, but I would hate to say where an authenticating postscript begins. As noted earlier, 4:10-23 was originally an independent letter, and the content is so personal that it suggests that it was all written in Paul's hand. Alternatively, we might assume that when the three letters were combined, they were inevitably edited, and in the process autograph sections might have been omitted, because authenticity was not a problem and/or the content was not significant.

3

Collecting the Letters

Despite the very definite individuality of each of the Pauline letters, not a single one has been transmitted separately. Each has come down to us associated with others attributed to the apostle. How did the collection of Paul's letters come into being? The question has been debated intensely, but no consensus has emerged. On the contrary, there are two diametrically opposed hypotheses, the evolutionary theory of progressive development and the big bang theory of sudden appearance.

THE EVOLUTIONARY THEORY

The evolutionary theory is the older, and the solidity of its consensus is manifest in that the debate has resulted in the formulation of two only slightly different versions, one associated with the name of Adolf von Harnack and the other with that of Kirsopp Lake.

According to Harnack (1926, 6–27), the letters that Paul sent to various churches were treasured by their recipients from the very beginning. Even those who disagreed with him recognized their power and authority (2 Cor 10:10). Each community read its letter(s) publicly; they became, as it were, the basic charter of the local church. The authoritative claim of Paul's letters was so much part of the self-identity of his converts that those with a different perspective on Christianity to propose were forced to resort to forging letters purporting to come from the apostle (2 Thess 2:2; 3:17).

At this early stage, however, no community believed that its letters had any wider importance. They had been occasioned by a particular situation in an individual community, and insofar as they were part of its unique history they were irrelevant to other churches. Only in the last quarter of the first century did the conviction arise that the particularity of the letters enshrined principles and insights of universal importance (Dahl 1962). It was then that an effort was made to collect the surviving letters with a view to presenting the totality of Paul's work to the church.

The first collection comprised ten letters (Romans, 1 and 2 Corinthians, Galatians, Ephesians, Philippians, Colossians, 1 and 2 Thessalonians and Philemon), because only letters addressed to churches were sought. It was probably made at Corinth. Harnack drew attention to the generalizing address of 1 Corinthians, which in his view introduced the collection, and emphasized the fact that 2 Corinthians was itself a compilation. At that stage some who had known Paul personally acted as a control and as protection against the incorporation of forgeries. Sometime before the end of the century the collection was expanded to thirteen by the addition of the Pastorals. Late in the second century Hebrews was added, bringing the number up to fourteen.

In opposition to Harnack, Lake (1911, 356–58) maintains that the initial conviction of the value of Paul's letters would have sparked a desire to have as many letters as possible. Very early, therefore, each community would have requested copies from neighboring churches. In this way a number of local collections with differing contents grew up. Once such partial collections began to be compared, awareness of their circumscribed origin dictated a policy of addition for the sake of completeness rather than one of deletion for fear of forgery. Sometime in the second century it was recognized that all lists were identical in content even though diverse in order. At this point the Pauline canon closed.

A more specific form of this theory is put forward by H.-M. Schenke, who makes a Pauline "school" responsible for the collection and dissemination of the apostle's letters. The members of this school were a group of first- and second-generation disciples deeply concerned to preserve Paul's distinctive theology. They became not only the guardians of his teaching insofar as they preserved and reedited existing letters, but also the propagators of his doctrine inasmuch as they drew on their deep familiarity with Paul's mind to create in his name new letters better adapted to the changing circumstances of the Pauline churches. Once Paul's reputation was definitively established and the complete collection of "his" letters was accepted by the church in general, the school dissolved.

The Big Bang Theory

The first serious challenge to the evolutionary theory came from E. J. Goodspeed (1927, 1945). He argued that the initial postulate of his predecessors was anachronistic. Each of Paul's letters was written for an immediate practical purpose and, once it had made its point, it was forgotten. A church which thought its letter(s) might be needed for future reference preserved it/them in an archive, but there was no liturgical use or theological consultation. Other letters might have survived through sheer chance.

Thus the situation remained, until interest in Paul was stimulated by the publication of the Acts of the Apostles around A.D. 90. If in this work Paul was given more attention than Peter, his role in the establishment of Christianity must have been of great significance. It was a further step to considering Paul's writings as foundational. This was taken by an old man who had been a disciple of the apostle. He knew of the whereabouts of one or two letters and made a determined and ultimately successful effort to find all the others of which he had heard. He found Romans, 1 and 2 Corinthians, Galatians, Philippians, Colossians, 1 and 2 Thessalonians, and Philemon. When he published them as a collection, sometime in the last decade of the first century, he wrote Ephesians, which draws on all nine letters, as a synthesizing preface designed to highlight the force and insight of Paul's theology (Goodspeed 1933, 79–165).

J. Knox, followed by Mitton, developed this hypothesis further. He argued that, since Philemon is theologically trivial, the only explanation for its inclusion must be personal. It must have had special significance for the compiler, who also had a special affection for Colossians, which served as the framework for Ephesians. Presumably Colossians was the letter he knew best. Is it possible to be more specific? In the light of the letter of Ignatius to the Ephesians, written in the first decade of the second century, Knox answers in the affirmative, because the bishop named in that letter is called Onesimus. The editor of the Pauline corpus, Knox maintains, was the ex-slave mentioned in Philemon, a native of Colossae who owed his freedom to Paul and who as bishop had both the training to write Ephesians and the authority to promulgate the collection.

Goodspeed and Knox also discussed the principle of the establishment of the collection. The earliest list is that of Marcion (mid-second century), which is known only indirectly through the testimony of Tertullian (ca. 160–225) and Epiphanius (ca. 313–403). Though the two witnesses do not agree—compare Tertullian, *Adversus Marcion* 5.1.9; 5.21.1, and the two different lists in Epiphanius, *Panarion* 42.9.4 and 42.11.9–11—Knox assumes that Marcion's intention is preserved in Epiphanius' list. The order is Galatians, Corinthians, Romans, Thessalonians, Laodiceans (= Ephesians), Colossians, Philemon, Philippians. But if Ephesians was written as the preface, it should come first. So it did, Knox agrees, but Marcion relegated it to the place of Galatians when he moved Galatians to the beginning because its anti-Jewish thesis reflected his own preferences.

In order to solve the perplexing order of the letters, Knox appeals to the Marcionite prologues, brief introductions to the Pauline letters conserved in the Vulgate (for details see Clabeaux). Since there is only one prologue each for Corinthians and Thessalonians, he deduces that 1 and 2 Corinthians and 1 and 2 Thessalonians were treated as two letters and not as four. This would permit a descending order of length, were it not for Philemon, which should come after Philippians. We must assume, argues Knox, that Colossians and Philemon were so closely associated in the popular mind that they were treated as one letter. The original collection, therefore, was essentially made up of seven letters: Ephesians, Corinthians, Romans, Thessalonians, Galations, Colossians + Philemon, and Philippians. It became the inspiration of the seven letters which introduce Revelation (1:4–3:22), and of the seven letters which Ignatius, who became bishop of Antioch around A.D. 69, wrote as a prisoner on his way to execution in Rome (ca. A.D. 107).

W. Schmithals (1972, 239–74) also maintains that the Pauline collection was the achievement of a single editor at a given moment. He does not identify the editor by name, but insists on his motive, which was to provide the church with arms against the inroads of Gnosticism. His goal was to demonstrate that Paul always and everywhere opposed Gnostic ideas. To this end, we are told, the editor dismembered the Pauline letters and recombined the elements so that each of the resulting letters contained at least some anti-Gnostic polemic. It was also part of the editor's intention to break down the barrier of particularity and exhibit the relevance of the letters for the whole Church by ensuring that they were seven in number, namely, 1 Corinthians, 2 Corinthians, Galatians, Philippians, 1 Thessalonians, 2 Thessalonians, and Romans (in that order).

Schmithals' hypothesis has had no influence (Gamble 1975). His dissection of the letters is in no way restrained by objective evidence. Its entirely arbitrary character is of a piece with his erroneous judgment that Gnostic influences had a major impact on Paul's communities.

WAS PAUL INVOLVED?

When dealing with the functions of a first-century secretary, I drew attention to the proposal of Richards that "the first collection of Paul's letters were in codex form and arose from Paul's personal copies and *not* from collecting the letters from various recipients" (1991, 165 n. 169). Richards further suggests that the one responsible for the publication of the Pauline letters was Luke. The simplicity of this hypothesis is a strong point in its favor. It is also recommended by the ancient practice of retaining copies of letters sent. Against this hypothesis, however, is the fact that it cannot account for the letters which are made up of a number of originally independent letters (e.g., 2 Corinthians and Philippians). These would not have been combined in Paul's notebooks.

Without being aware of Richards' hypothesis, David Trobisch (1989, 129–31) has an answer to this objection. Galatians, he argues, was not the first letter Paul wrote, but it was the first to have an impact beyond the audience to which it was originally addressed. Not all its readers agreed with him, but those who did wanted to read more. This stimulated Paul's desire to give permanent expression to his teaching. At the same time his quiet life at Ephesus gave him the opportunity to develop into a systematic thinker. His first project was to distill from his correspondence with Corinth the series of reflections on pastoral problems which has survived as 1 Corinthians. The response was overwhelming. Paul became convinced that henceforth (cf. 2 Cor 10:10) his pastoral vocation should be realized in writing and not in speech.

This transformation was inhibited by trouble in Ephesus. Forced to leave the city, Paul began what he feared might be his last visit to his European communities. Partly in response to their demands, and partly because of his own desire to leave a definitive record, he revised and combined the letters he had sent to the different Churches. His stays at Thessalonica and Philippi resulted in 1 Thessalonians and Philippians. While at Corinth he combined four letters to produce 2 Corinthians. During the long winter there he found time to commit to paper the fundamentals of his theology. This general thesis later became known as Romans.

On his way to Jerusalem from Greece Paul met with a delegation from Ephesus to whom he gave copies of 2 Corinthians and Romans, having appended personal greetings to the latter. This was the nucleus of the first Pauline collection, which the Ephesians created by the addition of 1 Corinthians and Galatians, copies of which had been retained there. This subsequently inspired another collection, this time comprised of four letters of general interest, namely Romans, 1 Corinthians, Ephesians, and Hebrews (the last because chapter 13 was understood as Paul's recommendation of a work which had come into his hands in Rome).

At the beginning of the second century an influential Church leader prepared a complete collection of the extant letters. Trobisch follows Goodspeed in identifying him as Onesimus, bishop of Ephesus. For personal reasons Onesimus added Philemon to Ephesians, Philippians, Colossians and 1 and 2 Thessalonians, thus opening the door for the inclusion of other letters addressed to individuals, namely, 1 and 2 Timothy and Titus.

THE ORDER AND LENGTH OF THE LETTERS

What is striking in this brief summary of the history of research is the degree of speculation. This, of course, is a consequence of the dearth of evidence, and there are those who claim that, since nothing can be said with confidence, the problem should be ignored. Such defeatism is not espoused by many. Those who continue to attack the problem tend to stay within the framework of previous research by critiquing the existing theories in terms of the plausibility of their assumptions and the consistency and force of their internal logic. Any serious evaluation, however, must begin with a reexamination of what evidence there is. Such hard data is concentrated in two areas, the length of letters and their order in the earliest collections. Inadequate as they may be, these are the only bases for an answer to the questions: Which theory is the more probable? Is there a hypothesis which more adequately accounts for the data?

The Length of the Letters

In antiquity the customary manner of measurement of a text was by the *stichos*. The term means a row or line, as in a row of trees, a line of soldiers, or a line of writing. Hence the science of calculating the length of a text is called stichometry. It is not a modern invention.

P46 (ca. A.D. 200) notes the number of stichoi in five of the Pauline letters. The Codex Sinaiticus (fourth century) does the same for ten of the letters. Sometime in the fourth century "Euthalius" numbered the stichoi in the letters (Marchand 1956). The pioneering researches of Charles Graux and Rendell Harris determined that the average stichos contained fifteen to sixteen syllables or between thirty-four and thirty-eight letters. Their conclusions regarding the letters have been admirably summarized by Finegan (1956, 96) who is the source of the following table as regards stichoi and the letter count of Graux. To the latter I have added the computer letter count of Trobisch (1989, 138). The computer word count was provided by my student Alfred Noratto, O.P. (see also Aune 1987, 205).

The Length of the Pauline Letters

	Words	Letters Graux	Letters Trob.	Stichoi P46	Stichoi Sinai.	Stichoi Harris	Stichoi Euth.
Rom	7111	35266	34410	1000		942	920
1 Cor	6829	32685	32767			897	870
2 Cor	4477	21851	22280		612	610	590
Gal	2230	11202	11091	375[1]	312	304	293
Eph	2435	11932	12012	316	312	325	312
Phil	1629	7975	8009	225	200	218	208
Col	1582	7745	7897		300	215	208
1 Thes	1481	7468	7423			202	193
2 Thes	823	4011	4055		180	112	106
1 Tim	1591	8575	8869		250	239	230
2 Tim	1238	6554	6538		180	177	172
Titus	659	3595	3733		96	98	97
Phlm	335	1567	1575			42	38
Heb	4953	26738	26382	700	750	714	703

This order is that which has become traditional in printed Bibles. The only discernible pattern is that most of the letters are ordered by length.

The compiler could not organize the letters chronologically, because no Pauline letter was dated. Nor was there any precedent for an alphabetical order. Adoption of the codex form by Christians (an undisputed but still unexplained phenomenon) recommended the inscription of the longest letter first, followed by the others in decreasing order. A roll could always be extended, but not a sewn quire (see p. 5 above), and a book which ended with only half of a letter would be virtually unsaleable (Trobisch 1989, 112). There was also a precedent for ordering by decreasing length. The major and minor prophets of the Old Testament

---

[1] The number is quoted accurately from Finegan, but appears to be a mistake for 275.

are organized in this way. The principle was also applied subsequently. The different tractates within the six divisions of the Mishnah appear in order of decreasing length and so do the 114 surahs of the Koran (Aune 1987, 205).

A close examination of the traditional list, however, quickly reveals that there are a number of exceptions. If length, following the letter count of Trobisch, is made the sole criterion, the list appears as follows:

Rom 1 Cor *Heb* 2 Cor *Eph* Gal *1 Tim* Phil Col 1 Thess *2 Tim* 2 Thess Titus Phlm

In this version the four italicized letters occupy unconventional positions. Why were they assigned to the positions they in fact occupy in today's Bibles?

The Order of the Letters

The most thorough recent research into the order of the Pauline letters in the Greek manuscript tradition is that of David Trobisch, who found nine different arrangements (1989, 56). The first is represented by two ninth-century manuscripts (F 010 and G 012). The second and third are widely attested, but all the others appear in only one manuscript each. In the table on p. 123 a question mark means an incomplete manuscript.

The vast majority of manuscripts belong to Groups A and B, which, if we leave aside Hebrews, are distinguished only by the order of Philippians and Colossians. Which is likely to be the more primitive? Trobisch suggests (1989, 39, 58) that the original order based on length found in Group A was changed in order to associate Colossians closely with Ephesians, because the latter was identified by Marcion as the letter to the Laodiceans mentioned in Colossians 4:16, and appears under that name in the lists of his Pauline canon given by Tertullian and Epiphanius.

While not impossible, there may be a simpler explanation. Philippians is in fact longer. If we take the figures of Graux and Trobisch it has 7975/8009 letters against 7745/7897 for Colossians. In other words, Colossians is 99 percent of the length of Philippians. The difference is only 230/112 letters. It is not surprising that in the Euthalian table they both have 208 stichoi. In

The Order of the Pauline Letters

Group A				Group B				
1	2	3	4	5	6	7	8	9
Rom	Rom	Rom	Rom	Rom	Rom	Rom	Rom	Rom
							Heb	
1 Cor	1 Cor	1 Cor	1 Cor	1 Cor	1 Cor	1 Cor	1 Cor	1 Cor
2 Cor	2 Cor	2 Cor	2 Cor	2 Cor	2 Cor	2 Cor	2 Cor	2 Cor
Gal	Gal	Gal	Gal	Gal	Gal	Gal	Eph	Gal
								Heb
Eph	Eph	Eph	Eph	Eph	Eph	Eph	Gal	Eph
Phil	Phil	Phil	Phil	Col	Col	Col	Phil	Phil
Col	Col	Col	Col	Phil	Phil	Phil	Col	Col
1 Thess	1 Thess	1 Thess	1 Thess	1 Thess	1 Thess	1 Thess	1 Thess	1 Thess
2 Thess	2 Thess	2 Thess	2 Thess	2 Thess	2 Thess	2 Thess	?	2 Thess
		Heb	Heb		Heb			
1 Tim	1 Tim	1 Tim	1 Tim	1 Tim	1 Tim	1 Tim	?	?
2 Tim	2 Tim	2 Tim	2 Tim	2 Tim	2 Tim	2 Tim	?	?
Titus	Titus	Titus	Titus	Titus	Titus	Titus	?	?
Phlm	Phlm	Phlm	Phlm	Phlm	Phlm	Phlm	?	?
	Heb		Heb			Heb	?	?

the stichometric count of the Codex Sinaiticus, however, Colossians has 300 against 200 for Philippians. Finegan (1956, 80, 103) accepts the latter figure at face value, but I suspect that it is a scribal error for 300, because Codex Sinaiticus in fact places Philippians before Colossians. In any case, it is clear that a copyist had only to increase his script slightly in one case and diminish it in the other for the true order of Philippians and Colossians to be reversed. Moreover, it must also be kept in mind that Group B is represented only by the sixth century D 06 and the fourteenth century minuscule 5. Hence, the order Colossians before Philippians can be dismissed as an error without historical significance.

List 8 is that of P46 which is dated around 200. It is related to Group A in its ordering of Philippians-Colossians, but is distinguished from all others by its positioning of Hebrews after Romans, and Ephesians before Galatians. Trobisch postulates (1989, 60) that this came about through a combination of the first list in Group A with a collection containing Romans, Hebrews, 1 Corinthians, and Ephesians. I do not find this hypothesis convincing. The exclusion of 2 Corinthians is not explained. It is easy, however, to see what is going on. If 2 Corinthians is not discretely left aside at this point, it will create difficulties later when Trobisch (1989, 66–82) attempts to prove that there existed versions of Romans, 1 Corinthians, and Ephesians which contained no mention of Rome, Corinth, or Ephesus in their respective addresses. 2 Corinthians opposes this hypothesis.

Nor is any explanation provided for the placing of Hebrews immediately after Romans in P46. The problem, however, is not insoluble. To put Hebrews in its correct position (in terms of length) after 1 Corinthians would split up the Corinthian correspondence. The compiler had to chose between putting it before 1 Corinthians or after 2 Corinthians. Perhaps it was the doctrinal importance of Hebrews that made him opt for the former. The Sahidic version took the latter option (Anderson 1966, 432).

The inclusion of Ephesians in Trobisch's postulated list is, of course, designed to explain its position. I doubt that this hypothesis is really necessary. The difference in length between Galatians and Ephesians is very slight. Ephesians is, in fact, 730/921 letters longer than Galatians, which is a difference of 8 percent (Galatians is 92 percent the length of Ephesians), but the stichometry of the Codex Siniaticus makes them equal with 312 stichoi each. Thus the situation is parallel to that of Philippians-Colossians discussed above. It only needed a scribe to write slightly larger letters in one or smaller letters in the other for them to look the same length. It is entirely possible, therefore, that the inversion Ephesians-Galatians in this unique series (no. 8) is the result of a mistake in determining the length of each. It can be dismissed as an insignificant error.

The final list (no. 9), which is that of the Codex Vaticanus (mid-fourth century), is also related to Group A both by the order of the first four letters and that of the last three. The only anomaly is the position of Hebrews which here, in contrast to P46, tends to confirm the hypothesis that Romans, Corinthians, Galatians was at one stage an independent collection. If so, Hebrews was tacked on to it as a supplement. Alternatively one might consider that it was inserted as the lead of the other collection, Ephesians, Philippians, Colossians, Thessalonians.

The thrust of this discussion has been to deny any historical significance to certain listings whose order seems to have arisen through error. When corrected they can be aligned with others, reducing the number of variants from nine to six, as shown in the following table, which is an adaptation of that given by Trobisch (1989, 57; the heading numbers correspond to the lists in the previous table).

Revised Order of the Pauline Letters

1/5	2/7	3/6	4	8	9
Rom	Rom	Rom	Rom	Rom	Rom
				Heb	
1 Cor	1 Cor	1 Cor	1 Cor	1 Cor	1 Cor
2 Cor	2 Cor	2 Cor	2 Cor	2 Cor	2 Cor
Gal	Gal	Gal	Gal	Gal	Gal
					Heb
Eph	Eph	Eph	Eph	Eph	Eph
Phil	Phil	Phil	Phil	Phil	Phil
Col	Col	Col	Col	Col	Col
1 Thess	1 Thess	1 Thess	1 Thess	1Thess	1 Thess
2 Thess	2 Thess	2 Thess	2 Thess	?	2 Thess
		Heb	Heb		
1 Tim	1 Tim	1 Tim	1 Tim	?	?
2 Tim	2 Tim	2 Tim	2 Tim	?	?
Titus	Titus	Titus	Titus	?	?
Phlm	Phlm	Phlm	Phlm	?	?
	Heb		Heb		

Trobisch (1989, 62) explains all the different lists as various combinations of a thirteen-letter list with a hypothetical four-letter list made up of Romans, Hebrews, 1 Corinthians, and Ephesians. We have seen that this latter list is not necessary to explain the position of Ephesians in P46. Neither is there any justification for separating 1 and 2 Corinthians, nor for the excision of "at Corinth" from the address of 1 Corinthians. Far from being a general letter, its contents show 1 Corinthians to be a highly specific response to the problems of a particular Church. Moreover, in order to explain the addition of Hebrews, it is not necessary to postulate that it already belonged to a collection.

The salient feature is the varying position of Hebrews (Hatch 1936). Lists 1/5 and 2/7 are irrelevant because Hebrews does not appear in the first and occurs at the very end in the second. List 8 can be set aside as an adaptation of the position of Hebrews in list 9 in function of the principle of length. In the remaining lists (3/6, 4, and 9) Hebrews is consistently found in the same configuration; the preceding letter is always shorter than the succeeding letter. In other words, the position of Hebrews draws attention to breaks in the decreasing length pattern and unambiguously suggests the existence of three partial collections to which Hebrews was appended, namely,

Collection A	Rom 1 Cor 2 Cor Gal
Collection B	Eph Phil Col 1 Thess 2 Thess
Collection C	1 Tim 2 Tim Titus Phlm

CREATING THE COLLECTION

Before investigating these collections more closely, it is important to establish the time-frame. There is wide agreement that the thirteen letters in list 1/5 were known and acknowledged in the second century. The consensus is founded on the traces of Pauline literary influence which have been detected, with acknowledged varying degrees of probability, (1) in late New Testament works, namely, the Johannine corpus, Hebrews, 1 and 2 Peter, James, Jude, and (2) in early non-canonical Christian writings, namely, the Shepherd of Hermas, the Epistle of Barnabas, the Didache, in addition to the letters of Clement, Ignatius, and Polycarp (Barnett 1941; Spicq 1969, 160–70; Lindemann 1979). While not every author betrays the influence of each one of the letters, it is significant that none of these authors knows only one of the postulated three partial collections. Virtually everyone betrays an awareness of all three. It is difficult to avoid the conclusion that the thirteen/fourteen-letter corpus was in place around the turn of the century. The partial collections, therefore, must have come into being sometime in the last third of the first century.

The existence of the partial collections was suggested by literary evidence. To become probable, the hypothesis needs further support, because the arrangements possibly may have beeen due to other, random factors. The simplest test is geographical. Are the letters within a partial collection associated in terms of place of origin and/or place of reception?

Collection A

Romans was written from Corinth, to which 1 and 2 Corinthians were addressed. Galatians, on the contrary, was composed in Ephesus or Macedonia and sent to the center of Asia Minor. In order to bring Galatians within the orbit of the other three, however, one has only to assume that Paul brought to Corinth a copy of Galatians with a view to developing a fuller treatment of the role of Israel and the Law in the plan of salvation, which eventually took the form of Romans.

Other advantages flow from the hypothesis that this collection originated at Corinth. The stimulus may have been the discovery that letters, whose immediate purpose was long past, nonetheless contained principles and formulations of enduring value. This gave rise to editorial work on the part of the Church, which selected three letters addressed to it as worthy of conservation, namely, 1 Corinthians, 2 Corinthians 1–9 and 2 Corinthians 10–13, while abandoning the "previous letter" (1 Cor 5:9) and the "severe letter" (2 Cor 2:4) in the process. The exclusion of the latter is understandable. The former may have been lost before the importance of preservation was recognized. Perhaps this was also the reason why copies of 1 and 2 Thessalonians were not kept at Corinth.

The alternative candidate for where the letters were collected, Ephesus, is much less likely. Although Galatians was probably composed there, only 1 Corinthians was certainly sent from there. Romans and the two components of 2 Corinthians have nothing to do with Ephesus.

Collection B

Philippi and Thessalonica were neighboring churches linked by the Via Egnatia; they were only 103 miles apart (Rossiter 1981, 562). Each had received three letters from Paul. The Philippians combined theirs into one letter before exchanging them with the Thessalonians, who reduced theirs to two. Such an exchange is all the more natural given the missionary ethos these communities shared. Of all his foundations Paul saw only these two as exercising effective existential witness (1 Thess 1:6-8; Phil 2:14-16).

Philippi also had contacts with the churches of the west coast of Asia Minor. Polycarp, bishop of Smyrna, who was martyred around A.D. 155, wrote to the church at Philippi:

> You and Ignatius have both written to me to ask whether anyone who may be going to Syria could deliver a letter from you there along with ours. I will see that this is done; perhaps by myself personally if I can find a suitable opportunity, or else by someone whom I will send to act for both of us. I am sending you Ignatius' letters, as you requested; the ones he wrote to us and some others that we had in our possession (*Phil* 13.1-2; Staniforth 1968, 149).

The letters of Paul cannot have been accorded lesser value. If the letters of Ignatius were exchanged across the Aegean Sea, so were those of Paul.

Ephesians and Colossians are also closely associated in that the author of the former certainly knew the latter intimately. Colossae is 113 miles from Ephesus, but we do not know whence Colossians was written. Rome would perhaps be the choice of the majority, but hints in the letter rather suggest Ephesus, notably the request for lodgings in Colossae in Philemon 22, which suggests a first stop on release from prison. As Polycarp's letter shows, communications between Macedonia and the west coast of Asia Minor were good. Smyrna is only a good day's walk north of Ephesus. It would take another week to get to Troas (189 miles), where there was also a Pauline community (2 Cor 2:12-13) and then two days by ship to Neapolis and Philippi (Acts 16:11-12). Hence, an interchange of letters between Thessalonica/Philippi and Ephesus is both feasible and plausible. Whether the collection took place in the north or in the south is irrelevant, because the implication of the exchange is that both termini had all the available letters.

Collections A and B

The combination of the partial collections A and B could have taken place in two ways, either through a Corinth-Macedonia link or through a Corinth-Ephesus link. Both are equally possible.

Even during Paul's lifetime it is clear that he was not the only contact between Corinth and its sister churches to the north and east. He could not have proclaimed that the Thessalonians had become "an example to all the believers in Macedonia and Achaia" (1 Thess 1:7) unless Corinthian Christians had visited there and brought back a glowing report on the quality of life of the Church. One believer may even have been so impressed that he stayed, and was later sent back to Corinth to assist in the organization of the collection for the poor of Jerusalem (2 Cor 8:18; Murphy-O'Connor 1991b, 86). From Ephesus Chloe's people went on business to Corinth (1 Cor 1:11), and we can be sure that they were not the only ones. Equally, it would be most surprising if some Corinthian Christians had not gone on business to Ephesus.

No church which had gone to the trouble of editing its own letters and collecting others would have remained silent about its achievement in the presence of members of another church. The temptation to display superiority is deeply rooted in human nature, and in this case such boasting could be rationalized in two ways. It might lead to the acquisition of new letters and, if the others had not thought of making a collection, it might incite them to do so. Once again the inevitable consequence of the exchange would be an expanded collection for both participants.

Collection C

At this point it should be clear that the big bang theory does not account for what evidence there is. The different orders point to partial collections, which can plausibly be ascribed to geographic connections. It is equally apparent, however, that Lake's version of the evolutionary theory does not hold water, because the partial collections were only being formed when Hebrews appeared on the scene, sometime between 80 and 90. Manifestly it took time for the value of exchanges to be perceived. Once partial collections had made their mark the process speeded up, and nets were cast as widely as possible.

At this stage the inclusion of letters to individuals was practically inevitable. Ephesus had at this time a collection of nine letters. Knox, it will be remembered, postulated that it was the inclusion of Philemon by Onesimus, bishop of Ephesus, that opened the door for the addition of the three Pastorals. This is not the only possibility, however, as Guthrie pointed out (1966, 268).

According to 1 Timothy 1:3, Timothy was also bishop of Ephesus, and he too possessed a cherished letter; in my view 2 Timothy. It seems likely, however, that Timothy had left Ephesus while Paul was still alive. Although an excellent assistant, he proved to be much less successful as a church leader, and Paul wanted him out of there quickly (2 Tim 4:9, 21; Prior 1989, 155, 165). A further difficulty in postulating Timothy as the editor of the Pauline collection is the inclusion of the inauthentic 1 Timothy and Titus; unless he was their author, it is unlikely that he would have accepted them.

The exclusion of Timothy strengthens the case for Onesimus as the one responsible for the complete collection of Paul's letters. Moreover, his role is necessary to explain the presence of Philemon. Onesimus would have had little difficulty in accepting 1 Timothy and Titus, because Ephesus already knew of 2 Timothy, the letter which had withdrawn Timothy from their midst, and the others were superficially similar. How he came to know them is an open question. It seems unlikely that Timothy would have forgotten 2 Timothy at Ephesus, or that the community there would have insisted on making a copy. As we have seen, interest in conservation developed only after the death of the apostle.

Abbreviations

AB	Anchor Bible
AJ	Josephus, *Antiquities of the Jews*
ATR	*Anglican Theological Review*
Att	Cicero, *Letters to Atticus*
AusBR	*Australian Biblical Review*
AUSS	*Andrews University Seminary Studies*
BAGD	W. Bauer, W. F. Arndt, F. W. Gingrich, and F. W. Danker, *A Greek-English Lexicon of the New Testament and Other Early Christian Literature.* Chicago: University of Chicago, 1979
BDF	F. Blass, A. Debrunner, and R. W. Funk, *A Greek Grammar of the New Testament and Other Early Christian Literature.* Chicago: University of Chicago, 1961
BETL	Bibliotheca Ephemeridum Theologicarum Lovaniensium
BFCT	Beiträge zur Förderung christlicher Theologie
BHT	Beiträge zur historischen Theologie
BT	*The Bible Translator*
BZNW	Beihefte zur Zeitschrift für die neutestamentliche Wissenschaft
CBQ	*Catholic Biblical Quarterly*
CNT	Commentaire du Nouveau Testament
DBS	Dictionnaire de la Bible: Supplément

EBib	Etudes Bibliques
ExpTim	*Expository Times*
Fam	Cicero, *Letters to His Friends*
HNT	Handbuch zum Neuen Testament
HNTC	Harper's New Testament Commentaries
HTKNT	Herders theologischer Kommentar zum Neuen Testament
HTR	*Harvard Theological Review*
ICC	International Critical Commentary
JBL	*Journal of Biblical Literature*
JSNTSup	Journal for the Study of the New Testament, Supplements
JSOT	*Journal for the Study of the Old Testament*
JTS	*Journal of Theological Studies*
LCL	Loeb Classical Library
LSJ	H. G. Liddell, R. Scott, and H. S. Jones, *A Greek-English Lexicon.* Oxford: Clarendon, 1966.
MeyerK	H.A.W. Meyer, ed., Kritisch-exegetischer Kommentar über das Neue Testament
MRB	Monographische Reihe von 'Benedictina'
NICNT	New International Commentary on the New Testament
NJBC	New Jerome Biblical Commentary
NovT	*Novum Testamentum*
NovTSup	Novum Testament, Supplements
NTOA	Novum Testament et Orbis Antiquus
NTS	*New Testament Studies*
PW	S. Wissowa (ed.) *Paulys Real Enclopädie der classischen Aeterkumswissenschaft*
QFr	Cicero, *Letters to His Brother Quintus*
RB	*Revue Biblique*
RHPR	*Revue d'Histoire et de Philosophie Religieuses*
SBLDS	Society of Biblical Literature, Dissertation Series
SD	Studies and Documents
TDNT	G. Kittel and G. Friedrich, eds., *Theological Dictionary of the New Testament*
THKNT	Theologischer Handkommentar zum Neuen Testament
WBC	Word Biblical Commentary

WUNT	Wissenschaftliche Untersuchungen zum Neuen Testament
ZNW	*Zeitschrift für die neutestamentliche Wissenschaft*
ZSTh	*Zeitschrift für systematische Theologie*

Bibliography

Abbott, T. K. (1897). *A Critical and Exegetical Commentary on the Epistles to the Ephesians and to the Colossians.* ICC. Edinburgh: Clark.

Achard, G., trans. (1989). *Rhétorique à Herennius.* Budé. Paris: Belles Lettres.

Aletti, J.-N. (1990). "La présence d'un modèle rhétorique en Romains: Son rôle et son importance." *Biblica* 71, 1–24.

————. (1991). *Comment Dieu est-il juste? Clefs pour interpréter l'épitre aux Romains.* Parole de Dieu. Paris: Seuil.

————. (1992). "La *dispositio* rhétorique dans les épîtres pauliniennes: proposition de méthode." *NTS* 38, 385–401.

————. (1993). *Saint Paul. Epitre aux Colossiens.* EBib. Paris: Gabalda.

Allo, E.-B. (1956). *Saint Paul. Seconde Épitre aux Corinthiens* EBib. Paris: Gabalda.

Anderson, C. P. (1966). "The Epistle to the Hebrews and the Pauline Letter Collection." *HTR* 69, 429–38.

Archer, R. L. (1951–52). "The Epistolary Form in the New Testament." *ExpTim* 63, 296–98.

Askwith, E. H. (1911). " 'I' and 'We' in the Thessalonian Epistles." *Expositor* 8th series, 1, 149–59.

Audet, J.-P. (1958). "Esquisse historique du genre littéraire de la 'Bénédiction' juive et de l'"Eucharistie' chrétienne." *RB* 65, 71–99.

Aune, D. E. (1977). *The New Testament in Its Literary Environment.* Library of Early Christianity. Philadelphia: Westminster.

Bachmann, M. (1991). *Sünder oder Ubertreter. Studien zur Argumentation in Gal 2, 15ff.* WUNT 59. Tübingen: Mohr.

Bahr, G. J. (1966). "Paul and Letter Writing in the First Century." *CBQ* 28, 465–77.

_____. (1968). "The Subscriptions in the Pauline Letters." *JBL* 87, 27–41.

Bailey, C., trans. (1926). *Epicurus, the Extant Remains.* Oxford: Oxford University Press.

Bailey, D.R.S. (1971). *Cicero.* London: Duckworth.

_____, trans. (1982). Cicero, *Selected Letters.* London: Penguin.

Barclay, W. (1960–61). "Hellenistic Thought in New Testament Times: The Way of Tranquillity; The Epicureans." *ExpTim* 72, 78–81, 101–4, 146–49.

Barnett, A. E. (1941). *Paul Becomes A Literary Influence.* Chicago: University of Chicago Press.

Barrett, C. K. (1968). *The First Epistle to the Corinthians.* HNTC. New York: Harper & Row.

_____. (1973). *The Second Epistle to the Corinthians.* HNTC. New York: Harper & Row.

_____. (1987). *The New Testament Background: Selected Documents.* Rev. ed. San Francisco: Harper & Row.

Barth, M. (1984). "Traditions in Ephesians." *NTS* 30, 3–25.

Baumert, N. (1973). *Täglich sterben und auferstehen. Der Literalsinn von 2 Kor 4, 12–5.10.* Studien zum Alten und Neuen Testament 24. Munchen: Kosel.

Benoit, P., J. T. Milik, and R. de Vaux. (1961). *Les grottes de Murabba'at.* Discoveries in the Judean Desert 2. Oxford: Clarendon.

Berger, K. (1974). "Apostelbrief und apostolische Rede / Zum Formular frühchristlicher Briefe." *ZNW* 65, 190–231.

Betz, H. D. (1979). *Galatians. A Commentary on Paul's Letter to the Churches in Galatia.* Hermeneia. Philadelphia: Fortress.

_____. (1985). *2 Corinthians 8 and 9. A Commentary on Two Administrative Letters of the Apostle Paul.* Hermeneia. Philadelphia: Fortress.

Bjerkelund, C. J. (1967). *Parakalo: Form, Funktion und Sinn der Parakalo-Sätze in den paulinischen Briefen.* Oslo: Universitetsforlaget.

Bligh, J. (1969). *Galatians. A Discussion of St. Paul's Epistle.* London: St Paul's Publications.

Boers, H. (1975). "The Form-Critical Study of Paul's Letters: 1 Thessalonians as a Case Study." *NTS* 22, 140–58.

Bruce, F. F. (1982). *1 & 2 Thessalonians.* WBC 45. Waco, Tex.: Word Books.

Brunot, A. (1955). *Le génie littéraire de saint Paul.* Lectio divina 15. Paris: Cerf.

Bultmann, R. (1976). *Der zweite Brief an die Korinther.* MeyerK; ed. E. Dinkler. Göttingen: Vandenhoeck & Ruprecht.

Bünker, M. (1984). *Briefformular und rhetorische Disposition im 1. Korintherbrief.* Göttingen: Vandenhoeck & Ruprecht.

Butler, H. E., trans. (1920–22). Quintilian, *Intitutio Oratoria.* LCL. Cambridge: Harvard.

Canfield, C.E.B. (1982). "Changes of Person and Number in Paul's Epistles." *Paul and Paulinism. Essays in honour of C. K. Barrett.* Eds. M. D. Hooker and S. G. Wilson. London: SPCK.

Caplan, H., trans. *Rhetorica ad Herennium.* LCL. Cambridge: Harvard.

Carrez, M. (1980). "Le 'nous' en 2 Corinthiens. Paul parle-t-il au nom de toute la communauté, de groupe apostolique, de l'équipe ministérielle ou en son nom personnel? Contribution à l'étude de l'apostolicité dans 2 Corinthiens." *NTS* 26, 474–86.

Church, F. F. (1978). "Rhetorical Structure and Design in Paul's Letter to Philemon." *HTR* 71, 17–33.

Clabeaux, J. J. (1992). "Marcionite Prologues to Paul." *Anchor Bible Dictionary* 4:520–21. New York: Doubleday.

Conzelmann, H. (1975). *1 Corinthians.* Hermeneia. Philadelphia: Fortress.

Dahl, N. H. (1962). "The Particularity of the Pauline Epistles as a Problem in the Ancient Church." *Neotestamentica et Patristica.* NovTSup 6, 261–71. Leiden: Brill.

Deissmann, A. (1901). *Bible Studies. Contributions Chiefly from Papyri and Inscriptions to the History of the Language, the Literature, and the Religion of Hellenistic Judaism and Primitive Christianity.* Edinburgh: Clark.

Dobschütz, E. von. (1933). "Wir und Ich bei Paulus." *ZSTh* 10, 251–77.

Doughty, D. J. (1972–73). "The Priority of Charis. An Investigation of the Theological Language of Paul." *NTS* 19, 163–80.

Dunn, J.D.G. (1988). *Romans.* WBC 38. Dallas: Word Books, 1988.

Elliott, J. K. (1981). "The Language and Style of the Concluding Doxology at the end of Romans." *ZNW* 72, 124–30.

Ellis, E. E. (1978). *Prophecy and Hermeneutic in Early Christianity. New Testament Essays.* WUNT 18. Tübingen: Mohr.

————. (1986). "Traditions in 1 Corinthians." *NTS* 32, 481–502.

Eschlimann, J.-A. (1946). "La rédaction des épitres Pauliniennes d'après une comparaison avec le lettres profanes de son temps." *RB* 53, 185–96.

Fee, G. D. (1987). *The First Epistle to the Corinthians.* NICNT. Grand Rapids: Eerdmans.

Finegan, J. (1956). "The Original Form of the Pauline Collection." *HTR* 49, 85–103.

Forbes, C. (1986). "Comparison, Self-Praise, and Irony: Paul's Boasting and the Conventions of Hellenistic Rhetoric." *NTS* 32, 1–30.

Forbes, R. J. (1955). *Studies in Ancient Technology.* Vol. 3. Leiden: Brill.

Frame, J. E. (1912). *A Critical and Exegetical Commentary on the Epistle of St. Paul to the Thessalonians.* ICC. Edinburgh: Clark.

Francis, F. O. and J. P. Sampley. (1975). *Pauline Parallels.* Sources for Biblical Study 9. Philadelphia: Fortress; Missoula: Scholars Press.

Funk, R. W. (1967). "The Apostolic *Parousia*: Form and Function." *Christian History and Interpretation: Studies Presented to John Knox.* Ed. W. R. Farmer and others, 249–68. Cambridge: Cambridge University Press.

Furnish, V. P. (1984). *II Corinthians.* AB 32A. Garden City: Doubleday.

Gamble, H. (1975). "The Redaction of the Pauline Letters and the Formation of the Pauline Corpus." *JBL* 94, 403–18.

_____. (1977). *The Textual History of the Letter to the Romans. A Study in Textual and Literary Criticism.* SD 42. Grand Rapids: Eerdmans.

Gnilka, J. (1968). *Der Philipperbrief.* HTKNT 10/3. Freiburg: Herder.

Goodspeed, E. J. (1927). *New Solutions of New Testament Problems.* Chicago: University of Chicago Press.

_____. (1933). *The Meaning of Ephesians.* Chicago: University of Chicago Press.

_____. (1945). "The Editio Princeps of Paul." *JBL* 64, 193–204.

Graux, C. (1978). "Nouvelles recherches sur la stichométrie." *Revue de Philologie* 2, 97–143.

Gummere, R. M. trans. Seneca. (1953). *Ad Lucilium epistulae morales.* LCL. Cambridge: Harvard.

Guthrie, D. (1966). *New Testament Introduction. The Pauline Epistles.* London: Tyndale.

Hall, R. G. (1987). "The Rhetorical Outline for Galatians: A Reconsideration." *JBL* 106, 277–87.

Harnack, A. von. (1926). *Die Briefsammlung des Apostels Paulus und die anderen vorkonstantinischen christlichen Briefsammlungen.* Leipzig: Hinrich.

_____. (1928). "*Kopos (kopian, hoi kipiôntes)* im früchristlichen Sprachgebrauch." *ZNW* 27, 1–10.

Harris, R. (1893). *Stichometry.* London.

Hatch, W.H.P. (1936). "The Position of Hebrews in the Canon of the New Testament." *HTR* 29, 133–51.

Héring, J. (1949). *La première épitre de saint Paul aux Corinthiens.* CNT 7. Neuchatel and Paris: Delachaux & Niestlé.

Hofmann, K.-M. (1938). *Philema Hagion.* BFCT 2. Gütersloh: Mohn.

Hughes, F. W. (1989). *Early Christian Rhetoric and 2 Thessalonians.* JSNTSup 30. Sheffield: JSOT Press.

Hunter, A. M. (1961). *Paul and his Predecessors.* 2d ed. London: SCM Press.

Jay, P., trans. (1981). *The Greek Anthology and other Ancient Epigrams.* London: Penguin.

Jeremias, J. (1958). "Chiasmus in den Paulusbriefen." *ZNW* 49, 145–56.

Jewett, R. (1969). "The Form and Function of the Homiletic Benediction." *ATR* 51, 18–34.

_____. (1970). "The Epistolary Thanksgiving and the Integrity of Philippians." *NovT* 12, 40–53.

_____. (1986). *The Thessalonian Correspondence. Pauline Rhetoric and Millenarian Piety.* Foundations & Facets: NT. Philadelphia: Fortress.

_____. (1986). "Following the Argument of Romans." *Word-World* 6 382–89.

Kennedy, G. A. (1963). *The Art of Persuasion in Greece.* London: Longman, 1963.

_____. (1972). *The Art of Rhetoric in the Roman World.* Princeton: Princeton University Press.

_____. (1984). *New Testament Interpretation through Rhetorical Criticism.* Chapel Hill and London: University of North Carolina Press.

Ker, W.C.A. trans. Martial. (1919–20). *Epigrams.* LCL. New York: Putnam.

Klauck, H.-J. (1984). *1. Korintherbrief.* Neue Echter Bible 7. Wurzburg: Echter.

_____. (1986). *2. Korintherbrief.* Neue Echter Bible 8. Wurzburg: Echter.

Knox, J. (1935). *Philemon Among the Letters of Paul. A New View of Its Place and Importance.* Reprinted 1959. New York and Nashville: Abingdon Press.

Koskenniemi, H. (1956). *Studies zur Idee und Phraseologie des griechischen Briefes bis 400 n. Chr.* Helsinki: Akateeminen Kirjakauppa.

Lake, K. (1911). *The Earlier Epistles of St. Paul.* London: Rivingtons.

Lampe, P. (1992). "Aquila." *Anchor Bible Dictionary* 1:319–20. New York: Doubleday.

Lawson-Tancred, H., trans. Aristotle. (1991). *The Art of Rhetoric.* London. Penguin.

Lietzmann, H. (1949). *An die Korinther I–II.* HNT 9. Tübingen: Mohr.

Lincoln, A. T. (1990). *Ephesians.* WBC 42. Dallas: Word Books.

Lindemann, A. (1979). *Paulus im ältesten Christentum.* BHT 58. Tübingen: Mohr.

Lofthouse, W. F. (1946–47). "Singular and Plural in St. Paul's Letters." *ExpTim* 58, 179–82.

————. (1952–53). " 'I' and 'We' in the Pauline Letters." *ExpTim* 64, 241–45.

————. (1955). " 'I' and 'We' in the Pauline Epistles." *BT* 6, 72–80.

Lohr, C. H. (1961). "Oral Techniques in the Gospel of Matthew." *CBQ* 23, 403–35.

Lohse, E. (1968). *Die Briefe an die Kolosser und an Philemon.* MeyerK. Göttingen: Vanderhoeck & Ruprecht.

Longenecker, R. N. (1990). *Galatians.* WBC 41. Dallas: Word Books.

Lund, N. W. (1942). *Chiasmus in the New Testament. A Study in Formgeschichte.* Chapel Hill: University of North Carolina.

Lyons, G. (1985). *Pauline Autobiography: Towards a New Understanding.* SBLDS 73. Atlanta: Scholars Press.

Mack, B. L. (1990). *Rhetoric and the New Testament.* Minneapolis: Fortress.

Malherbe, A. (1977). "Ancient Epistolary Theorists." *Ohio Journal of Religious Studies* 5, 3–77.

Marchand, J. W. (1956). "Gothic Evidence for 'Euthalian Matter.' " *HTR* 49, 159–67.

Martin, R. P. (1986). *2 Corinthians.* WBC 40. Waco, Tex.: Word Books.

Merklein, H. (1992). *Der erste Brief an die Korinther. Kapitel 1–4.* Okumenischer Taschenbuchkommentar zum Neuen Testament 7/1. Gütersloh: Mohn; Würzburg: Echter.

Milik, J. (1953). "Une lettre de Siméon Bar Kokheba." *RB* 60, 276–94.

Mitchell, M. (1991). *Paul and the Rhetoric of Reconciliation. An Exegetical Investigation of the Language and Composition of 1 Corinthians.* Hermeneutische Untersuchungen zür Theologie 28. Tübingen: Mohr.

Mitteis, L. (1908). *Romisches Privatrecht bis auf die Zeit Diokletians.* Leipzig: Duncket & Humbolt.

Mitton, C. L. (1955). *The Formation of the Pauline Corpus of Letters.* London: Epworth.

Mullins, T. Y. (1963). "Petition as a Literary Form." *NovT* 5, 46–64.

————. (1964). "Disclosure as a Literary Form in the New Testament." *NovT* 7, 44–50.

————. (1968). "Greeting as a New Testament Form." *JBL* 87, 418–26.

————. (1972). "Formulas in New Testament Epistles." *JBL* 91, 380–90.

————. (1972–73). "Ascription as a Literary Form." *NTS* 19, 194–205.

————. (1973). "Visit Talk in New Testament Letters." *CBQ* 35, 350–58.

_____. (1977). "Benediction as a New Testament Form." *AUSS* 15, 59–64.

Murphy-O'Connor, J. (1964). *Paul on Preaching.* New York: Sheed & Ward.

_____. (1966). "Paul: Philippiens (Épitre aux)." DBS 7. Paris: Letouzey & Ane, 1211–33.

_____. (1979). "Food and Spiritual Gifts in 1 Cor 8:8." *CBQ* 41, 292–98.

_____. (1982). *Becoming Human Together. The Pastoral Anthropology of Saint Paul.* Good News Studies 2. Wilmington, Del.: Michael Glazier.

_____. (1986). "Interpolations in 1 Corinthians." *CBQ* 48, 81–94.

_____. (1986). "Pneumatikoi and Judaizers in 2 Cor 2:14–4:6." *AusBR* 34, 42–58.

_____. (1988). "Philo and 2 Cor 6:14–7:1." *RB* 95, 55–69.

_____. (1990). "The Second Letter to the Corinthians." NJBC 50. Englewood Cliffs, N.J.: Prentice Hall, 816–29.

_____. (1991). "2 Timothy Contrasted with 1 Timothy and Titus." *RB* 98, 403–18.

_____. (1991). *The Theology of the Second Letter to the Corinthians.* NT Theology. Cambridge: Cambridge University Press.

_____. (1992). *St. Paul's Corinth. Texts and Archaeology.* Good News Studies 6; 2d ed. expanded. Collegeville, Minn.: The Liturgical Press.

O'Brien, P. T. (1977). *Introductory Thanksgivings in the Letters of Paul.* NovTSup 49. Leiden: Brill.

_____. (1987). "Ephesians 1: An Unusual Introduction to a New Testament Letter." *NTS* 25, 504–16.

Olson, S. (1984). "Epistolary Uses of Expressions of Self-Confidence." *JBL* 103, 585–97.

_____. (1985). "Pauline Expressions of Confidence in His Addressees." *CBQ* 47, 282–95.

Paton, W. R. trans. (1939). *The Greek Anthology.* LCL. Cambridge: Harvard.

Pearson, B. A. (1971). "1 Thessalonians 2:13-16: A Deutero-Pauline Interpolation." *HTR* 64, 79–94.

Perrin, B., trans. Plutarch. (1967–70). *The Parallel Lives.* LCL. Cambridge: Harvard.

Pesch, R. (1986). *Paulus ringt um die Lebensform der Kirche. Vier Briefe an die Gemeinde Gottes in Korinth.* Freiburg: Herder.

Plummer, A. (1915). *A Critical and Exegetical Commentary on the Second Epistle of St. Paul to the Corinthians.* ICC. Edinburgh: Clark.

Prior, M. (1989). *Paul the Letter-Writer and the Second Letter to Timothy.* JSNTSup 23. Sheffield: JSOT Press.

Probst, H. (1991). *Paulus und der Brief. Die Rhetorik des antiken Briefes als Form der paulinischen Korintherkorrespondenz (1 Kor 8–10).* WUNT 2/45. Tübingen: Mohr.

Prümm. K. (1960). *Diakonia Pneumatos. Der zweite Korintherbrief als Zugang zur apostolischen Botschaft.* Vol. 2/1. Rome: Herder.

Rackham, H., trans. Pliny. (1944). *Natural History.* LCL. Cambridge: Harvard.

Radice, B., trans. Pliny. (1969). *Letters and Panegyricus.* LCL. Cambridge: Harvard.

Rawson, E. (1975). *Cicero.* London: Penguin.

Refoule, F. (1990). "A contre-courant Rom 16, 3–16." *RHPR* 70, 409–20.

Richards, E. Randolph. (1991). *The Secretary in the Letters of Paul.* WUNT 2/42. Tübingen: Mohr.

Rieu, E. V., trans. Homer. (1963). *The Iliad.* London: Penguin.

Roberts, C. H., and T. C. Skeat. (1983). *The Birth of the Codex.* 2d ed. London: Oxford University Press.

Roberts, J. H. (1986). "Pauline Transitions to the Letter Body." In *L'apôtre Paul. Personnalité, style et conception du ministère.* BETL 73, ed. A. Vanhoye. Leuven: Peeters.

Robinson, J.A.T. (1962). *Twelve New Testament Studies.* Studies in Biblical Theology 34. London: SCM Press.

Robinson, J. M. (1964). "Die Hodajor-Formel in Gebet und Hymnus des Fruhchristentums." *Apophoreta: Festschrift für Ernst Haenchen.* Ed. W. Eltester and F. H. Kettler. Berlin: Töpelmann.

Roetzel, C. (1969). "The Judgement Form in Paul's Letters." *JBL* 88, 305–12.

Rolfe, J. C., trans. Suetonius. (1979). *Lives of the Caesars.* LCL. Cambridge: Harvard.

Roller, O. (1933). *Das Formular der paulinischen Briefe. Ein Beitrag zur Lehre vom antiken Briefe.* Stuttgart: Kohlhammer.

Rossiter, S. (1981). *Greece.* Blue Guide, 4th ed. London: Benn.

Sanders, J. T. (1962). "The Transition of Opening Epistolary Thanksgiving to the Body in Letters of the Pauline Corpus." *JBL* 81, 348–62.

———. (1966). "First Corinthians 13. Its Interpretation since the First World War." *Interpretation* 20, 159–87.

Sass, C. (1941). "Zur Bedeutung von *doulos* bei Paulus." *ZNW* 40, 24–32.

Schenke, H.-M. (1975). "Die Weiterwirken des Paulus und die Pflege seines Erbs durch die Paulusschule." *NTS* 21, 505–18.

Schlier, H. (1962). *Der Brief an die Galater*. MeyerK. Göttingen: Vandenhoeck & Ruprecht.

Schmithals, W. (1964). "Die Thessalonischerbriefe als Briefcompositionen." *Zeit und Geschichte: Dankesgabe an Rudolf Bultmann*. Ed. E. Dinkler, 295-315. Tübingen: Mohr.

————. (1972). "On the Composition and Earliest Collection of the Major Epistles of Paul." In idem, *Paul and the Gnostics*. Nashville: Abingdon.

Schnider, F., and W. Stenger. (1987). *Studien zum neutestamentlichen Briefformular*. New Testament Tools and Studies 11. Leiden: Brill.

Schubert, P. (1939). *Form and Function of the Pauline Thanksgivings*. BZNW 20. Berlin: Topelmann.

Skeat, T. C. (1979). "Especially the Parchments: A Note on 2 Timothy IV.13." *JTS* 30, 172-77.

Smit, J. (1989). "The Letter of Paul to the Galatians: A Deliberative Speech." *NTS* 35, 1-26.

Smith, R. F. (1981). "Chiasm in Sumero-Akkadian." *Chiasmus in Antiquity. Structures, Analyses, Exegesis*. Ed. J. W. Welch, 17-35. Hildesheim: Gerstenberg Verlag.

Spicq, C. (1969). *Saint Paul, Les Epitres Pastorales*. EBib; 2d ed. Paris: Gabalda.

Standaert, B. (1978). *L'évangile selon Marc. Composition et genre littéraire*. Nijmegen: Stichting Studentenpers.

————. (1983). "Analyse rhétorique de chapitres 12 à 14 de 1 Co." *Charisma und Agape (1 Ko 12-14)*, MRB 7. Ed. L. De Lorenzi, 23-34. Rome: St. Paul's Abbey.

————. (1986). "La rhétorique ancienne dans saint Paul." *L'apôtre Paul. Personnalité, style et conception du ministère*, BETL 73. Ed. A. Vanhoye, 78-92. Leuven: Peeters, 1986.

Staniforth, M., trans. (1968). *Early Christian Writings. The Apostolic Fathers*. London: Penguin.

Stowers, S. K. (1986). *Letter-Writing in Greco-Roman Antiquity*. Library of Early Christianity 5. Philadelphia: Westminster.

————. (1985). Review of Betz, 1985 *JBL* 106 (1987) 727-30.

Taatz, I. (1991). *Frühjüdische Briefe. Die paulinischen Briefe im Rahmen der offiziellen religiosen Briefe des Frühjudentums*. NTOA 16. Freiburg: Universitätsverlag; Göttingen: Vandenhoeck & Ruprecht.

Trobisch, D. (1989). *Die Entstehung der Paulusbriefsammlung*. NTOA 10. Freiburg: Universitätsverlag; Göttingen: Vandenhoeck & Ruprecht.

Vaux, R. de. (1973). *Archaeology and the Dead Sea Scrolls*. London: Oxford University Press for the British Academy.

Vouga, F. (1988). "Zur rhetorischen Gattung des Galaterbriefes." *ZNW* 79, 291-92.

Watson, D. F. (1988). "A Rhetorical Analysis of Philippians and its Implications for the Unity Question." *NovT* 30, 57-88.

————. (1989). "1 Corinthians 10:23-11:1 in the Light of Greco-Roman Rhetoric: The Role of Rhetorical Questions." *JBL* 108, 301-18.

Weichert, V. (1910). *Demetrii et Libanii qui ferunter TYPOI EPISTO-LIKOI et EPISTOLIMAIOI CHARACTERES.* Leipzig: Teubner.

Weiss, J. (1910). *Der erste Korintherbrief.* MeyerK. Göttingen: Vandenhoeck & Ruprecht.

Welch, J. W. (1981). "Chiasmus in the New Testament." *Chiasmus in Antiquity. Structures, Analyses, Exegesis.* Ed. J. W. Welch, 211-49. Hildesheim: Gerstenberg.

————. "Chiasmus in Ancient Greek and Latin Literatures." *Chiasmus in Antiquity,* 250-68.

Westermann, W. L. (1928). "On Inland Transportation and Communication in Antiquity." *Political Science Quarterly* 43, 364-87.

White, J. L. (1971). "Introductory Formulae in the Body of the Pauline Letter." *JBL* 90, 91-97.

————. (1972). *The Body of the Greek Letter.* SBLDS 2. Cambridge, Mass.: Society of Biblical Literature, 1972.

————. (1984). "New Testament Epistolary Literature in the Framework of Ancient Epistolography." *Aufstieg und Niedergang der römischen Welt,* 2.25.2, 1730-56. Berlin: de Gruyter.

————. (1986). *Light from Ancient Letters.* Foundations & Facets: NT. Philadelphia: Fortress.

Widman, M. (1979). "1 Kor 2:6-16. Ein Einspruch gegen Paulus." *ZNW* 70, 44-53.

Williams, W. G., trans. (1926-29). Cicero, *Letters to His Friends.* LCL. Cambridge: Harvard.

————. (1953). Cicero, *Letters to His Brother Quintus.* LCL. Cambridge: Harvard.

Windisch, H. (1924). *Der zweite Korintherbrief.* MeyerK. Göttingen: Vandenhoeck & Ruprecht.

Winstedt, E. O., trans. (1912-18). Cicero, *Letters to Atticus.* LCL. Cambridge: Harvard.

Wolff, C. (1989). *Der zweite Brief des Paulus an die Korinther.* THKNT 8. Berlin: Evangelische Verlaganstalt.

Wuellner, W. H. (1976). "Paul's Rhetoric of Argumentation in Romans: An Alternative to the Donfried-Karris Debate over Romans." *CBQ* 36, 330-51.

_____. (1979). "Greek Rhetoric and Pauline Argumentation." *Early Christian Literature and the Classical Tradition.* Ed. W. R. Schoedel & R. L. Wilken, 177–88. Paris: Editions Beauchesne.

_____. (1986). "Paul as Pastor. The Function of Rhetorical Questions in First Corinthians." *L'apôtre Paul. Personnalité, style et conception du ministère,* BETL 73. Ed. A. Vanhoye, 49–77. Leuven: Peeters, 1986.

_____. (1987). "Where is Rhetorical Criticism Taking Us?" *CBQ* 49, 448–63.

Indices

CLASSICAL LITERATURE

146 Indices

DIO CHRYSOSTOM

Discourses
37:36   40

GREEK ANTHOLOGY
6:63   2
6:65   2
6:227   3
6:295   4, 5

HOMER

Iliad
4:299   88

MARTIAL

Epigrams
14:7   36
14:38   3
14:208   9

PAPYRI
P46   5, 123

BGU
2:423   56

PColZen
1:6   40

PLond
42   57

PMich
8:490   40
8:499   39

PMur
164   11

POxy
1:264   110
1:724   12

2:300   99
4:476   99

PRyl
2:231   99

UPZ
1:66   111

PLATO

Phaedo
264C   87

PLINY THE ELDER

Natural History
7:91   9
13:68-83   4
16:157   3

PLINY THE YOUNGER

Letters
3:5.15   13
3:5.17   13
9:36.2   10

PLUTARCH

Cato Minor
23:3-5   11
23:5   9

PSEUDO-DEMETRIUS

Typoi Epistolikoi
4:5-11   96

PSEUDO-LIBANIUS

Epistolimaioi Charactēres
15:16–17.1   96

New Testament

SUBJECTS